A Taoist Cookbook

A TAOIST COOKBOOK

With Meditations Taken from the Laozi Daode Jing

by Michael Saso

Charles E. Tuttle Co., Inc.
Boston • Rutland, Vermont • Tokyo

Published by Charles E.Tuttle Company, Inc. of Rutland, Vermont, and Tokyo, Japan, with editorial offices at 153 Milk Street, Boston, Massachusetts 02109

Library of Congress Cataloging-in-Publication Data

Saso, Michael R.
A Taoist cookbook : recipes with meditations from Lao-Tzu / by Michael Saso
p. cm.
Includes index.
ISBN 0-8048-3037-1
1. Cookery, Chinese. 2. Vegetarian cookery. 3. Taoist Meditations. I. Title.
TX724.5.C5S27 1994
641.5'636'0951—dc20 94-3126
CIP

Book and cover design by Lisa Diercks

The cover illustrations are from a set of late Qing (ca. 1890) dynasty lithographs and woodblocks depicting scenes from the life of the famous Quanzhen Taoist Yang Lairu.

First Edition
1 3 5 7 9 10 8 6 4 2
Printed in the United States (EB)

Acknowledgments

To my mother Beatrice, who let me use the study of Periwinkle in Carmel to type this; my daughters Theresa and Maria, who suffered my cooking; the young Tibetan scholar Baima, who brought me to Kumbun monastery; the Mongol shaman scholar Nima; A-ji, who let me stay at his home in Ürümqi and with whom we drove through the deserts of Xinjiang; Gu Lijun, who puts us up in Yinquan, Ningxia; to Wang Naidan and Wang Naiqing for their illustrations; Dennis Wyszynski for proofreading and correcting the manuscript; the many people who sampled these dishes in my Suyuan apartment in Beijing; the generous people of Yuanxuan Xueyuan in Kowloon; and to Shi Daochang of Mao Shan, my deepest gratitude.

Table of Contents

A List of the Illustrations

The illustrations that accompany the meditations were taken for the most part from a late Qing (Ch'ing) dynasty woodblock collection called the *Huitu Lidai Shenxian Juan* (Illustrated Biographies of the Immortals). The work, bound into eight small *juan* pamphlets, was reprinted in Shanghai in 1908 by the Saoye Shanfang Press from woodblocks stored in a private collection. The style of the woodblock carvings is typical of mid-Qing, popular devotional prints and *shanshu* (books published and read for good merit). The charming illustrations show men and women equally practicing and teaching Taoist meditation, while (almost always) serving a meal, a drink of tea, or welcoming a passerby.

Another group of illustrations are taken from the sketchbooks of two young Beijing artists, Wang Naidan and Wang Naiqing. After reading the recipes and meditations, they drew the ink drawings that appear throughout the book.

1. Laozi (Lao-tzu) leaves behind the *Daode Jing*, before entering the mountains.
2. Kong Yuanfang returned from old age to youth by eating magic mushrooms.
3. Lan Bianho stayed youthful by singing and dancing.
4. Wang Baochang used music to heal illness.
5. Huang An riding a two-thousand-year old turtle.
6. Wang Lieh ate *huangjing* (sealwort, a Chinese herbal remedy) to stay young.
7. Taoist Wang Zuan receives Taoist esoteric books on meditation.

8. Water is best of all.

9. Zhou Mu Wang dines with Mother Goddess of the West (Xi Wang Mu).

10. Two-hundred-year old Taoist Li Ran is not harmed by flames or ice.

11. Tao Hongjing, scholar and ninth master of Taoist Mao Shan.

12. Confucian scholar Cui Wei visits Taoist masters of Mt. Qingcheng, Sichuan.

13. Ho Shang Gong showing disciples how to meditate on Laozi.

14. Peng Zu, China's Methusela, lived for nine hundred years and still looked young.

15. Xu Xuanping, a Taoist recluse, lived in the hills and wrote poetry.

16. Lan Gong, a master of Taoist alchemy and breathing meditation.

17. Wei Boyang, author of a book on internal alchemy called *Cantongqi*.

18. Zhao Qu's skin disease was healed by three Taoist herbalists.

19. Han Emperor Wu blessed by female Taoist spirits.

20. Wang Yao, a Taoist healer, lives and meditates in the mountains.

21. Yuan Ji is told by a Taoist sage to respect nature and not kill wild animals.

22. Xiao Shi plays the flute, the wind spirit comes to listen.

23. Zuo Ci gives a Taoist banquet.

24. Don't stand on tiptoe too long.

25. Ya Shuqing learns recipes for health and long life.

26. The light of heart are rooted in peace.

27. Tang Ruoshan travels to Mt. Hua to practice the Taoist way of life.

28. Zhang Lao, one of the Eight Immortals, is visited by Taoist spirits.

29. Yang Wengbuo is led to spring water on a mountain top.

30. Hu Gong making wine on an alchemist's furnace.

31. Si Mingjun, Lord of the Kitchen Stove, records our good and bad deeds.

32. Pei Chen's recipes bring good health and long life.

33. Mao Meng learned Taoist recipes, then went to Mt. Hua to meditate.

34. Su Zishun maintained his youthful strength for 300 years on Taoist herbs.

35. Tao attracts all creatures to itself.

36. Chi Jian transmits Taoist teachings to his disciples.
37. Du Ziqun, vowing to follow Laozi's way, is fed by Taoist spirits.
38. Dong Feng gives up a high government post for Taoist meditation.
39. Zeng Qixu practices Buddhist and Taoist meditation.
40. Wen Kuangtong teaches Laozi in the mountains.
41. Ye Fashan learns *Zhengyi* (Dragon Tiger), a Taoist meditation.
42. Cai Yao heals illness with herbs on Qingcheng Mountain.
43. Zhang Zifang receives secret books from the Lord of the Yellow Stone.
44. Tea is served before a Taoist blesses a newborn child.
45. Fei Guanqing invites Taoist spirits to a banquet.
46. Taoist immortals attend Xie Zhao's banquet.
47. Masters Tao and Yin dine on Mt. Hua.
48. Act like Tao.
49. Wang Yuanzhi, 10th master of Taoist Mao Shan.
50. Chen Anshi, protector of animals, receives books from Taoist immortals.
51. Kong Anguo lived for three hundred years on Taoist alchemical recipes.
52. Yang Buochou studied the *Yijing* (*I-ching*) on Mt. Hua.
53. Zhang Guo, one of the Tang Dynasty (619–906) Eight Immortals.
54. Dong Fang Shuo, a Han dynasty scholar turned Taoist recluse.
55. Yin Gui, a Taoist alchemist, healer, and savant.
56. Zhou Ma, a Mt. Hua Taoist, healer and counselor.
57. Cui Qianyu, a healer, subdued and protected wild animals and nature.
58. Wang Qiao meditates, and wild ducks descend.
59. Jie Xiang is taught internal alchemy by a female Taoist immortal.
60. Guo Ziyi, a retired soldier, learns to meditate from Taoist immortals.
61. The hermit of Heng Shan lived on mountain herbs.
62. The ten Wei Yang friends retired to the mountains to practice Tao.
63. Huang Guanfu, a female Taoist, heals ills with vegetarian recipes.

64. Peng Qiu learns meditation from Taoist women in the mountains.
65. Ma Ziran ("Nature" Ma) invites guests to a banquet.
66. Cui Shanxuan, aTaoist poet.
67. Yang Zhenbuo learns from female Taoist spirits.
68. Xu Xiyan, a Confucian scholar, learns meditation from female Taoists.
69. Cui Wei receives a fiery message from immortal Taoist women.
70. My words are easy to know.
71. Pei Xuanjing, a Taoist master, entertains her guests.
72. Master Li teaches an "emptying" meditation in a Taoist garden.
73. Feng Daliang treats guests to a Taoist banquet.
74. Shen Bin is visited by Taoist immortals while meditating.
75. Qi Zhaoyao receives Laozi's *Daode Jing* from a Taoist immortal.
76. Heng Kai is carried to Peng Lai Island by an immortal heron.
77. Taoist immortals banquet on Mt. Song.
78. The soft overcomes the hard.
79. Cai Shaoxia is visited by a Taoist immortal.
80. The Taoist way is at one with nature.
81. Heaven's Tao gives without harm or discord.

Preface

Taoism (pronounced "Daoism") is the native-born religion of China. Unlike the West, where religions are defined by belief in a revealed scripture, the role of Chinese religion is to provide festive ritual for the year-long changes in nature and the life-cycle of humans. That is, Chinese religion highlights practice over belief.

In the West it would be unthinkable to belong to more than one religion, because Western religions demand that the believer adhere to one system of beliefs rather than another. Thus, one could not be Jewish, Islamic, and Christian at the same time. The Chinese, on the other hand, hold that life should be celebrated in one way, and death in another. There must be a religion that celebrates life and nature, and another that accomodates death and the afterlife. (The reader should note that until the influence of the West, the Chinese, like most other Asians, firmly believed in the existence of the soul or spirit after death). Confucianism provides ethical guidelines for social relationships. Buddhism teaches about releasing the soul in the afterlife, Taoism about life and nature.

These three religious practices make up a single Chinese culture. The mind, in this three-part system, is for thinking and judging, the heart for willing and loving, and the belly for intuitive wisdom as well as for digestion. Taoism is therefore the "religion of the belly."

This cookbook provides eighty-one recipes for good and harmonious life, along with eighty-one brief meditations about humans living in harmony with nature. The meditations are short paraphrases of the *Laozi Daode Jing* (*Lao-tzu Tao-te Ching*), one of the basic texts of Taoism. The reader is invited to try each recipe after meditating on the meaning of its Taoist text.

The idea of meditating and then cooking comes from watching Taoists in China, Taiwan, and Hong Kong, who used these recipes after quiet prayer and meditation. The Taoist believes that the body, heart, and mind must be in harmony with nature's changes in order to be healthy. Eating is a part of the cycle of yang and yin, day and night, summer and winter, that nature itself follows. Meditating helps keep us in harmony with nature, and eating meets the body's needs.

Before beginning the meditations and preparing the recipes, consider the meaning of Taoist words. Words for the Taoist are like nets or snares that capture the feelings, experiences, and intent of the speaker. Once the rabbit or fish is caught, the snare can be put aside. Once the meaning is understood, the word can be discarded. The meditations from the *Daode Jing* (*Tao-te Ching*) help us to understand nature's way by discarding the worrisome words that inhibit our health and digestion. We are told to be like nature, empty and giving. Only when empty can we receive from and be useful to others.

A number of special Taoist words are used in the meditations. Their meanings are described here for those unfamiliar with Taoist terminology. I have spelled out the Chinese Taoist words in the modern pinyin romanization, then in the nineteenth-century Wade-Giles writing system. Thus, *Laozi Daode Jing* in modern pinyin is spelled *Lao-tzu Tao-te Ching* in nineteenth- and early twentieth-century dictionaries. Here is a brief list of Taoist terms:

Daoism (Taoism) • The folk religion of China. Some Western and Asian scholars distinguish Taoist philosophy from Taoist religion. In the Taoist way of thinking, there is no such distinction.

Dao (Tao) • The ultimate, transcendent gestator of the cosmos.

wuwei (wu-wei) • The ultimate, transcendent Tao's "non" act of gestating. Thus the Dao of gestation is call *wuwei zhi* (jr) Dao.

de (te) • The intimate, immanent mother Dao (Tao) of nature. The immanent mother Dao of nature is also called *taiji* (*t'ai-chi*), *yuanqi* (*yüan-ch'i*), Primordial Breath, *hun-dun* (*hun-tun*), Undifferentiated Chaos.

yuwei (yu-wei) • The immanent, pregnant Dao, hanging on, "holding." The transcendent Dao "lets go," while the immanent mother Dao of nature "hangs on." Pregnant, it gestates yin and yang.

yang • The male, active, daylight, warring aspects of nature.

yin • The female, passive, night time, peacefully birthing nature.

qi (ch'i) • Primordial breath, intellect, life energy.

shen • Primordial spirit, will, love, heart, ruler of the body.

jing (ching) • Wisdom, emotions, the gut-level belly instincts. Head, chest, and belly in humans correspond to heaven, earth, and the watery underworld in nature.

meditation • Using the belly to pray, rather than the head to think distracting thoughts or the heart to wish selfish desires.

Introduction

The Taoist way of cooking was developed in the mountains, hills, and villages of China. Taoist monks and nuns living a solitary life, and lay Taoists living by the household fireplace, are all its progenitors. For them, Taoist cooking is a simple way of maintaining good health, long life, and well-being.

I found these recipes while traveling to Taoist monasteries, mountains, and households on the Chinese mainland, in Hong Kong, and in Taiwan, and practiced them while living in the quiet, peaceful way of a Taoist. Whether living alone as mountain recluses, with others in a monastic community, or surrounded by children in a village household, Taoists all emphasize the need to follow a simple way of life and to maintain healthy eating habits in harmony with the changes of nature. Good eating habits must be accompanied by good thoughts and healthy exercise. No matter how nutritious the food, it cannot be digested unless the mind's thoughts, the heart's desires, and the body's well-being are sound.

The art of Taoist cooking is therefore based on two principles: (1) simple, good food and (2) a simple, good life. The foods chosen are for the most part vegetarian. Meat, fish, eggs, alcohol, monosodium glutamate, cheese, and fats are avoided. However, those who eat meat are not condemned for doing so. If meat or fish is served at a banquet, the Taoist will take a little so as not to offend the host. When guests are toasted, the Taoist will also take a sip of wine or beer but otherwise will not indulge in heavy spirits. Should guests come to a Taoist monastery, meat, fish, and wines of all sorts may be served. This is because the guest is always made to feel at home. As a guest, I was invariably given a choice of pork, beef, shrimp, and other popular dishes, because most guests who visit Taoist mountains are used to ordinary Chinese or foreign tourist fare. Since I have tried for the past decade to follow a strict Taoist diet, as found in such Taoist places as Yuanxuan Xueyuan of Hong Kong, Mao Shan in Jiangsu, and other places, I avoided such items, choosing to eat what the Taoists themselves eat. However, it was obvious that guests were given whatever good things they desired to have and were available.

The Taoists of Mao Shan (sixty kilometers southeast of Nanjing in Jiangsu Province) kept a supply of canned pork, beef, shrimps, 110-proof Gaoliang (sorghum) liquor, and other delicacies requested by cadres (government officials) and other Party members who came on inspection tours. Though the Taoists themselves never ate or drank any of these things on their own, and absolutely forbade the use of monosodium glutamate (MSG; Mandarin: *weijing*) in their own diet, the cook provided these items for visiting cadres and scholars who asked for a fancy banquet.

There are two sound reasons for this practice. The first is that it would be quite contrary to the traditional Taoist way to alter any eating habit, or to convert anyone, foreigner or Chinese. The banquet table is not the place to teach, change others' behavior, or appear "holier than thou" in ascetic or health practice. The attitude of the Taoists is one of gracious welcome, no matter what the beliefs or customs of the guest.

The second reason for providing guests with the opportunity to enjoy large quantities of alcohol is for the practical purpose of inducing a happy state of euphoria in the Religious Affairs Bureau, Communist Party cadres, foreign and Chinese scholars, and others who come inquiring after Taoist affairs. The meditations and other esoterica of Taoism are passed on privately from master to disciple, or parent to child. My request to enter the Taoist kitchen, talk with the cooks, ask after Taoist prayer and healing methods, was frequently granted after those who did not follow Taoist ways and habits were happily sleeping after a sumptuous lunch.

Taoist monks, nuns, and recluses who follow the strictest rules of Taoist cooking, (sometimes called "macrobiotics," in the West) observe an almost pure vegetarian diet. In the rigorous monastic regimen all sorts of vegetables, legumes (beans), grains, fruits, and herbs are grown and eaten. Monastics practice daily Taoist meditation, which involves visualizing the breathing process, focusing on Tao present in the "center," and physical exercise. Taoists make a point of walking up and down mountain paths and stairways, and chanting or reading Taoist texts before meals. Things to be avoided in general include all worldly associations such as reading newspapers, watching television, and the thinking or expressing of negative thoughts and judgments of any sort that involve dispute or argument. Only positive topics are discussed when preparing Taoist meals.

Taoist vegetarian rules differ from those of monastic Buddhism. A strict Buddhist diet excludes garlic, onions, and spices, and never allows the eating of meat, fish, or animal products of any sort, including gelatin, milk, or cheese (with rennet). Taoist practices encourage the use of garlic for good health and allow the Taoist to eat small quantities of light meat or white fish at a banquet or when recovering from an illness. The Taoist diet allows the use of white rice, bread, and noodles (without eggs), contrary to Western books on macrobiotics, which forbid white starches. It also allows the use of "foreign" vegetables such as tomatoes ("foreign eggplant") and broccoli.

When consuming meat or wine, Taoists, like other Chinese culinary experts, do not ingest rice or other starches. Rice, noodles, and bread are taken separately from meat, fish, or alcohol, after the drinking has ended. Meat and starch, when taken together with alcohol, increase obesity and intoxication, and impede digestion.

Taoists who live a monastic or reclusive life are usually strictly vegetarian. Married Taoists, who fulfill the role of priest for China's folk religion, follow a strict vegetarian diet only when performing village rites of passage. These rituals include healing, burials, blessings, and the grand festival of village renewal called *Jiao* (*Chiao*), a rite of cosmic renewal. The vegetarian diet is thought to purify the mind, heart, and body before ritual and meditation.

While adhering to a vegetarian diet, many Taoists do eat roast or barbecue lamb when dining with Uighur, Hui, or other Islamic peoples of China. They also eat *tsampa* (highland roast barley mixed with *dri* [yak] butter and tea), yogurt, and small pieces of lamb meat in noodles when dining with Tibetans, as guests of the Nyingmapa "Redhat" and other Tantric Buddhist monks who frequently invite their guests to stay in the monastery, eat, and pray.

Lay Taoists who live at the Yuanxuan Xueyuan monastic complex of Samdiptam, New Territories (Hong Kong), eat whatever foods are served at banquets outside the monastic grounds, but follow the stricter Taoist diet when on retreat in the monastery, or when performing rituals. Married (hearth-side) Taoists of

Fukien, Zhejiang, Taiwan, Singapore, and Hong Kong (wherever Chinese communities are found) do not observe a strict Taoist diet except when performing rituals. Nevertheless, there are those among the Taoist masters of the villages of China who follow a strict vegetarian diet, a tradition passed down from antiquity.

It is physically evident from those who follow the Taoist diet and way of life that sufficient protein or amino acids are ingested from the proper combination of rice, legumes, corn, green vegetables, and dofu (tofu, bean curd). Should a doctor advise that some meat or fish be eaten, the Taoist rule insists that the doctor's counsel be followed. The same rule is used for medicines. Both Western and Chinese medicine, as prescribed by the patient's doctor, is taken.

I advocate all of the above practices; that is, a vegetarian diet is normally to be chosen, except when one is invited to a banquet, when guests come, or when the family doctor prescribes otherwise.

It is always the custom to serve a Taoist meal after reading, meditating on, or performing a Taoist text. Each recipe included in this cookbook comes with a brief meditation, in the form of a phrase taken from the great Taoist classic, the *Laozi Daode Jing* (*Lao-tzu Tao te Ching*), Lao-tzu's "Classic for Attaining the Tao." There are eighty-one meditations in the *Daode Jing* and eighty-one recipes in this cookbook. The reader is invited to use any recipe in combination with any other.

In China a restaurant meal usually consists of four dishes and one soup, five courses in all. Each evening meal should include one starch (rice, noodles, steamed or baked bread), three vegetable dishes with protein, and one fruit. Breakfast is a part of the well-rounded Taoist diet for the home, and several suitable recipes are included here. A well-functioning body in harmony with nature's changing seasons is a Taoist idea. Balanced, good cooking is essential to fulfilling this model.

The purpose of the this book is to describe a method of cooking, eating and meditating that is meant to bring about good health, long life, and contentment. Its ways are tested and proven, and can be used or adapted by anyone. The fact that it brings good health, happiness, and vitality is proven by the Taoist men and women in their late seventies and eighties who move vigorously up and down the hills and pathways of the Taoist hillside monasteries in Hong Kong and mainland China, nourished only by these recipes.

A Taoist Cookbook

Where the Recipes Were Gathered

I visited Taoists in many places to study their cooking, including the Xining area of Qinghai Province (northeastern Tibet), the Xinjiang Silk Road, various Taoist mountains and temples of mainland China, the Yuanxuan Xueyuan Taoist center of Samdiptam, the New Territories, near Hong Kong, the temples in and around the city of Hsinchu (Xinzhu), Taiwan, and the city of Beijing where I have lived since 1990. The recipes are presented in the order in which I learned them. They were used again and again, for the many guests who came to my apartment in the Haidian district of Beijing. Tasters and critics included Tibetans and Uighurs from the Minzu Xueyuan (Academy of the "Nationalities"), Han Chinese from The People's University (Renmin Daxue), Beijing University, and other nearby communities. Dishes that were pleasing to both Western and Asian palates were chosen.

Yuanxuan Xueyuan, a lay Taoist monastery

Located in the New Territories, Kowloon, Hong Kong, the Yuanxuan Xueyuan (Cantonese: Yunyun Hakyun) is organized and managed by a group of laymen and -women. The laymen and -women who patronize the temple follow the meditations and liturgies of the Quanzhen (Ch'üan-chen), All True, Taoist tradition. Quanzhen Taoism was founded in the late Song and early Mongol Yuan dynasties (twelfth to thirteenth centuries). It was originally meant to be a monastic celibate way of life for men and women equally and flourishes in the People's Republic of China today. All True Taoists practice Confucian ethics, Zen (Buddhist) sitting meditation, and Taoist breathing meditation. Married men and women can also follow the Quanzhen way of life, as can be seen at the Yuanxuan Xueyuan monastery. People from throughout Hong Kong and Kowloon come here to bury the dead, pray for the health and well-being of the living, and enjoy the excellent vegetarian dishes prepared daily in the temple dining hall.

On my first visit, the vegetarian restaurant provided an exquisite gourmet dinner for visiting Chinese and foreign scholars attending a Taoist conference at the Chinese University of Hong Kong. Vegetarian sweet-sour fish (see the sweet potato recipes), Tofu chicken, wheat gluten "pork" and "beef," a variety of sautéed vegetables, noodles, and fresh fruit were served. I was also deeply moved by the rituals of the lay Taoist association, performed equally by men and women.

I went to Hong Kong in the late summer of 1986, to learn more of lay Taoist life. Immediately upon my arrival, a simple vegetarian meal was laid out in welcome, consisting of vegetables with noodles, dofu, mushrooms, and fruit. Parts of the months of August and September were spent in the Yuanxuan Xueyuan community, during the performance of the grand Pudu (P'u-tu) rite for "Opening the Gates of Hell," and "Freeing All Souls" celebrated annually during the Seventh Lunar Month. (August-September in the Western calendar). I lived in the monastery compound, attended the rituals, recorded the music, and shared three meals a day with the Taoists. When not in strict ritual seclusion, Mr. Zhao Zhendong, the director of the monastery, drove us down to a dim sum restaurant in Tsuenwan, or to the Hilltop Country Club on a neighboring hill, where ordinary Chinese meat and fish dishes were served. The observance of Taoist cooking rules while in the monastery, and the occasional enjoyment of ordinary food in a Chinese restaurant, was the rule followed by these lay Taoists.

The basic principles of Taoist cooking taught at Yuanxuan Xueyuan were the adequacy and health-bringing qualities of a pure vegetarian diet, coupled with the ability to accept any other kind of food when dining out.

Mao Shan, a Taoist monastery near Nanjing, central China

Mao Shan is one of the most scenic Taoist mountains in China. Rising abruptly from the central Jiangsu plains forty miles southeast of Nanjing, its three peaks can be seen from miles away. Named after three brothers who meditated there between 160 B.C.E. and 140 B.C.E., during the early Han dynasty, it became the home of Shangqing (Shang-ch'ing), Highest Pure, Taoism in the fourth century C.E. Shangqing contemplative Taoism was founded by a woman named Wei Huacun. Scholars and emperors patronized the mountain and its eminent Taoists, and it became famous for its meditation manuals, rituals, and healing. A fifth- to sixth-century court scholar named Tao Hongjing (T'ao Hung-ching) collected and edited its scriptures. When a Song-dynasty empress had a fish bone stuck in her throat, a Mao Shan Taoist named Liu Hunkang extracted the deadly bone with a talisman.

The Japanese First Army burned the temples and executed more than fifteen hundred Taoists in January and February of 1938. The Red Guard destroyed what was left of the mountain retreat during the cultural revolution between 1966 and 1978. But with the return of some religious freedom in 1980, the peasants from the lowlands began rebuilding the monasteries and temples with small donations.

On the slope of second Mao Shan, there is an ancient monastery where young Taoists are trained in the music, rituals, and meditations of the Highest Pure tradition. A vegetarian diet is followed here, far more authentic than that at the tourist-oriented temple atop Great Mao Shan peak. The Temple of Ten Thousand Blessings (Wanfu Gong) atop the highest Great Mao Shan is surrounded by peddlars, photographers, and tourist buses. Chinese restaurant-style meals can be arranged for in the temple dining hall.

I made a total of seven trips to Mao Shan between 1986 and 1990, in order to study the rituals, music, meditations, and daily life of the monks. Much of the food eaten at the hillside monastery is grown there, while the food served to visitors at the summit of Great Mao Shan is carried by truck, cart, or hand. The Taoist meals consisted mostly of vegetables, legumes, dried and fresh fruit, and steamed white rice. An aging Taoist master named Shih Daochang (Shih Tao-ch'ang), who passed away in the spring of 1989, acted as host and instructor at the hillside monastery. It is his instructions, for the most part, that appear in the text.

Wudang Shan, the home of Taoist martial arts

From Nanjing or Shanghai I took the Yangtze River ferry upstream for a three- or four-day trip to Wuhan City in Hubei Province, and from there rode an overnight train to the city of Shiyan (Shih-yen) on the Hubei-Shaanxi border. To get to Wudang Shan from Shiyan required a five-hour bus ride through stunningly beautiful scenery that brought me into the high hills of the Purple Cloud Temple, where the Wudang Shan monasteries begin. A three-hour walk along the mountain paths and terraced hillsides leads to hermitages, shrines, and the Wudang summit temple, where a copy of the Taoist scriptures is kept. The Red Guard did not reach this beautiful spot, and so the magnificent temples and statues funded by Ming-dynasty emperors (1368–1644) remain intact.

As at Mao Shan, state-sponsored Quanzhen All True Taoists have taken over the official running of the Purple Cloud Temple. Authentic Taoist monastic and recluse life is found in the caves and shrines along the pathway to the summit, and an excellent Taoist meal is served by the Taoist caretaker. Taoists of the Beiji, Pole Star, tradition practice martial arts and meditation and grow their own vegetables. More than a thousand pilgrims a day come to this distant shrine of the martial arts dedicated to the spirit of the pole star, Xuantian Shangdi, patron of the Ming-dynasty emperors.

Lunghu Shan, Dragon-Tiger Mountain monastery in Sanqing Gong (San-Ch'ing Kung)

The headquarters of Zhengyi (Dragon-Tiger) Taoism, Lunghu Shan is the home of the first religious Taoist movement called the Zhengyi Celestial Master sect. Lunghu Shan or Dragon-Tiger mountain and its lakes are in southern Jiangxi (Chiang-hsi) province, a few miles from the border of Fujian province. Zhengyi Taoism was founded at the end of the Han dynasty between 145 and 215 C.E. From that time, when Cao Cao (Ts'ao Ts'ao) founded the Wei Kingdom in north China, until today, Zhengyi Taoism has had a profound and lasting influence on Taoism as a religious healing movement.

Wang Xiaolin, present ritual master of Dragon-Tiger Mountain, heir to the Wang clan position, was my host during a stay at the Sanqing temple. I was offered lunch by the 65th Celestial Master's mother, who provided a marvelous meal of corn, green vegetables, rice, and a river fish caught especially that morning for Wang Xiaolin, who had been ill. The aging Taoist enjoyed the fish, while the rest of us did justice to the other dishes. Rice with legumes, corn, and green vegetables, the Taoist's mother pointed out, provided protein readily usable for the body, whereas the fat in meat could do harm. The cooking of a fish was thought to be a remedy for Taoist Wang's cold.

Qingcheng monastery, a Taoist shrine in Sichuan

The famous Qingcheng, Green Wall Mountain, monastery is a three-hour bus ride from the bustling city of Chengdu in Sichuan. Taoists from the state-sponsored Quanzhen, All True, sect and the Taoist association collect fees at the shrines. One can ask for vegetarian food at the many wayside restaurants. However, Chinese restaurant-style meat and fish dishes are served to most of the thousands who visit the shrine daily from all over China. Tibetan Buddhist monks and Uighur Islamic pilgrims are among those who climb the mountain daily to pray before the ancient shrines.

Taoist cooking in Taiwan

One of the most important places to learn about Taoist cooking is at the grand festival of village renewal called Jiao (Chiao). Deriving from an ancient word meaning to offer incense, wine, and foods at a rite of passage (such as marriage), the name came to be used exclusively for the rite of village renewal celebrated by the fire-dwelling Taoists of southeast China (Fujian, Guangdong, and Taiwan). The festival is especially popular in modern Taiwan. Taoists are invited to celebrate a three- or five-day renewal, during which time the whole village follows a strict Taoist vegetarian diet. No living thing may be slaughtered, and foods from animals, including fish and milk, may not be ingested from the first to the last day of the ritual. Only on the afternoon of the last day, for the Taoist rite of amnesty for "freeing all souls from hell-purgatory" (P'u-tu), are animals slaughtered and used as a sacrificial offering. The Buddhist version of this rite, called Yulan Pen (Yü-lan P'en), offers vegetarian food as a banquet to free the souls. A vegetarian diet is followed throughout the festival because, in the teaching of the Taoist masters of Taiwan, a vegetarian diet is thought to keep the whole village as well as the Taoist pure for an encounter with the Tao, the transcendent gestator of the cosmos.

During the ritual the Taoists sing the forty-second chapter of the *Laozi Daode Jing:*

The Tao gave birth to the One,
The One gave birth to the Two,
The Two gave birth to the Three,
The Three gave birth to the Myriad
Things.

Tao is the gestator, the wu, the empty transcendent. One is breath, the yu, the motherly, pregnant aspect of nature. Two is yang, the male, active element of visible reality; and Three is yin, the female or passive element of visible reality. One, Two, and Three together gestate heaven, earth, and the watery-fiery underworld.

During the Jiao festival the Taoist communicates with the heavenly Tao by offering sweet things, wine, fire, flowers, precious items. The Tao of nature, earth mother, is offered chopped and cooked vegetarian foods. The lost souls suffering in an afterlife of watery or fiery hell are offered raw meats, slaughtered on the last day of the village Jiao festival. The orphaned and lost souls freed from the nine-tiered prison of hell come to the bloody meat offerings of the Jiao festival, which have been laid out whole and uncooked in front of the temple. The souls are "offered" raw, uncooked meat, to be "taken home" and prepared there for a banquet.

The Silk Road and a Tibetan temple of Qinghai

There are more than sixty-five nationalities within the confines of greater China. The fifty-one language and culture groups in the Tibetan-Burmese-southwest China area are matched in diversity by the Altaic and Turkish language groups of the desert Silk Road in northwest China. With the exception of the Mongols who follow Tibetan tantric Buddhism with overtones of primitive shamanism, the Altaic-Turkish cultural areas of the Silk Road are for the most part Islamic. The Uighur nationality, along with Kazakhs, Izbeks, Tajiks, Hui, and others, are famous for a vegetarian noodle dish that I have included in this book. This noodle dish can be found from Beijing to Ürümqui, in Xinjiang, the far northwest of Chinese Turkestan. The recipe included here comes from an exquisite Islamic restaurant near the Islamic mosque of Turfan.

There is no account I know of that does justice to the richness and diversity of culture, cuisine, and natural beauty found along the ancient silk road between Beijing and Si'an in China, and Tibet or Xinjiang to the far west. After visiting Sichuan in west China, my research took me to Beijing, and subsequently by train to Qinghai, northeast Tibet, through Inner Mongolia and Ningxia, Islamic China.

The food of Tibet is some of the most nourishing, strength-giving, and interesting in China. At Kumbun monastery (Chinese: Taer-si) in the high Huangnan grasslands I enjoyed the art, meditations, and dishes of Tibetan monastic life. *Tsampa* (roast highland barley mixed with yak [dri] butter and tea), barley bread, yogurt, and vegetables with noodles are included in this book as part of the Qinghai vegetarian diet.

Taoist and Buddhist monasteries from Lanzhou in Gansu Province to the Qinghai Province highlands enjoy this style of eating.

Traveling with my younger daughter Mari, we stayed in Kumbun as guests of the Abbot of the art college, a slight, gentle, humorous monk noted for his sculptures made from dri butter, called "mar." (The reader is reminded that the word yak means bull in Tibetan, whereas dri means a long-haired cow. Thus there is no such thing as yak butter or yak milk, unless bulls should be found that give milk in Tibet).

The temple fare consisted of fresh vegetables, tsampa, yogurt, barley bread, and tea prepared in the Tibetan style. Of special interest was the tsampa, a roll-like cereal made of roast highland barley flour mixed with Tibetan tea and dri butter, a little salt, and grated cheese for flavor. A bowl of tsampa enabled one to travel all day at the 12,000 foot altitude without feeling weak or dizzy.

Getting Ready

Taoist recipes are simple and easy to prepare. Those who are unfamiliar with Asian cooking may want to stock up on some basic ingredients and articles needed before embarking on the first meal. Here are some essentials:

Special items from the Asian section of a supermarket

1. A bottle of low-salt soy sauce (Japanese or Chinese style)
2. Dried and canned mushrooms, of any and all varieties
3. Nuts, including peanuts, walnuts, almonds, sunflower seeds
4. Plum sauce, sweet-sour sauce, etc.
5. Dried fruits, including apricots, dates, raisins
6. Dried sesame seeds, and sesame paste, if desired
7. Soybean paste, *doujiang* in Chinese, *miso* in Japanese
8. Chinese black peppercorns, *huajiao*, which are milder than the ordinary black pepper found in supermarkets
9. Chinese stir-fry or teriyaki sauce
10. Canned or fresh bamboo shoots
11. Canned water chestnuts
12. A package of fresh dofu (tofu), which keeps for only a few days, or preserved dofu in a bottle or box.

Vegetables and other items found in any supermarket

1. Polyunsaturated cooking oil (canola, for example)
2. Sesame oil
3. All sorts of green vegetables, including cabbage (Chinese, napa, bok choy [*bai tsai*] spinach, or broccoli. Any green vegetable can be prepared Chinese style, as can green bell peppers, corn, eggplant, carrots, and tomatoes.
4. A little salt to use occasionally when frying, to keep the hot oil from splashing. This can be omitted for those on low-salt diets. Generally, salt is avoided.
5. Potatoes of all sorts, sweet

potatoes, white potatoes, yams, the small Japanese *araimo*, taro root.

6. Roots of all sort: small and giant radish (Japanese *daikon*); onions of all sorts, small, large, white, and red; scallions; garlic and garlic shoots; the onion grass called *jiucai* (*chiu-ts'ai*) or chives.

7. Beans of all sorts, including packages of eight beans, "eight precious things" or fifteen kinds of beans, as a fine source of protein; peas, string beans, snow peas.

8. Any and all sorts of fresh fruit.

9. Rice, usually a daily staple, unless one choosed noodles.

10. Noodles made without eggs (see homemade noodle recipes), see-through noodles (Jpn. *harusame*), barley noodles (Jpn. *soba*); other starches, including baked or fried bread.

11. Sugar.

12. Vinegar (mild or Chinese brown vinegar).

Spices to keep on the shelf

1. Mustard seed, powdered and whole (*jiezi, chieh-tzu*)

2. Curry powder

3. Turmeric, or saffron if possible

4. Cumin (Silk Road cumin for best taste)

5. Oregano, basil, laurel, for making Silk Road spaghetti (recipe 69)

6. Chinese five-spice powder

7. Cinnamon

8. Garlic powder

Special foods to provide for guests

1. Beef, pork, shellfish, butter (do use yak [dri] butter where available), eggs, cheese, milk.

2. For occasional use when preparing a banquet or in times of illness: chicken with no fat, salt-water fish.

Pans and utensils

1. A nonstick frying pan or a wok with a lid. A Chinese frying pan has a rounded, not a flat, bottom, which uses less oil and cooks vegetables more evenly.

2. A large pot for boiling noodles.

3. A medium-sized pot with a tight lid for cooking rice, or an electric rice cooker, which cooks rice automatically.

4. A medium-sized pot for steaming vegetables, boiling stew.

5. A kettle for boiling water.

6. Two teapots, one for green and one for black tea.

7. A medium-sized pot for making Tibetan tea.

8. A large, sharp knife for chopping vegetables Chinese style.

9. Large wooden chopsticks, wooden spoons, a spatula.

10. A small electric oven for baking if you do not have a conventional oven.

Plates, saucers, utensils, chopsticks in sets of five (five represents the cyclic changes of nature)

1. Five large plates
2. Five small plates
3. Five cups and saucers
4. Five small soup bowls
5. Four serving plates and one serving bowl
6. Chopsticks
7. Five knives, forks, spoons, serving spoons.
8. Five glasses for juice, water, or wine for guests

The reader is reminded that the Taoist rule allows for the recipes to be changed to suit the tastes of the user. For example, it is often suggested that salt be put in the wok with cooking oil to keep the oil from splattering as it heats. In all recipes the salt may be omitted for those on a low-or nonsalt diet. If desired, a little chopped ginger or other spice can be used to season in its place. For the convenience of guests, salt and pepper shakers should be placed on the table. Monosodium glutamate should never be used. Meat may be mixed with many of the vegetable dishes, in the Chinese style. When meat can be used in a recipe, it will be mentioned. One may use more or less garlic, spice, oil, or combinations of various vegetables according to taste. The rule in all cases is to make a dish that is nourishing and tasty.

Getting Started

Chinese cooking is usually done in a round-bottomed frying pan called a wok, over a gas or charcoal flame. The secret of cooking well in such a small and "limited" environment is to heat the wok, add a little oil, and after 30 seconds or so, when the oil begins to smoke a bit, throw in the spices, then the vegetables, and stir for about a minute. Then reduce the flames, add some light soy sauce or a bit of water for steaming, and cover with a lid to simmer for another 3 or 4 minutes, or until lightly done. The oil coats the vegetables and keeps in the flavor. The vegetables are never allowed to overcook. They must remain crisp and fresh to the taste. As a final touch, simply thicken the broth by using a bit of cornstarch and sauce for flavor.

Many homes today come with electric stoves that do not allow for a quick regulation of heat. This problem can be overcome by using two burners, one at high heat to be used for the first minute and a half, the other at medium heat for simmering. In this manner a gas, charcoal, or electric stove can be used for preparing the Taoist dishes. The round-bottomed wok fits perfectly over the flames of a gas burner, but it is harder to manage on a flat surface. A regular frying pan can also be used in this case, without too much difference in procedure. It is better, however, not to use a Teflon or "stick-proof" pan, since the heat required in the beginning of the cooking process is often greater than Teflon, SilverStone, or other chemical coatings can survive. Chips of the coating come off in the food or during washing. A new metal frying pan or a wok can be made to function as a non-stick surface by coating the bottom with oil the first few times it is used and simply letting it bake into the metal surface. Empty the smoking hot oil out of the pan, run cold water for a moment over the surface (it will sizzle and steam), then return it to the stove, adding fresh oil. With the exception of stainless steel, almost any kind of metal can be made into a non-stick surface by using this method.

Some Chinese Taoist recipes are prepared by boiling and steaming. When the recipes call for steaming, a number of methods can be used, as long as the rule of not overcooking is followed. A wok or a frying pan can be used for steaming or boiling by adding a little water and covering it with a tight-fitting lid. A medium-sized pot can also be used, and the food placed on a circular steamer about an inch above the surface of the boiling water. A circular collapsible metal steamer is sold in many markets for this purpose. Many cooks simply use the wok for boiling or steaming as well as frying.

Meditations and Recipes

Tao

The Tao that is spoken is not the eternal Tao.
The name that is named is not the eternal name.
Wu, the letting-go Tao, is heaven and earth's origin;
Yu, pregnant Tao, is nature's mother.
Always let go, Wu, to know Tao's mystery,
Always hold on, Yu, to know Tao's presence. . . .

How to Cook Rice

White rice is used as a staple food throughout most of Asia. The first thing a cook does is wash the rice five or six times in running water, to remove the starch or powder around the rice kernel before cooking. Rice is cooked in the following manner: after washing, put the rice in the bottom of a pot with a tight lid. Some recipes call for measuring twice the amount of water as rice put in the pot, that is, 1 cup of rice, 2 cups of water. The cooks in the Taoist monastery followed a simpler rule. Pour in enough water to cover the rice to the first joint on the index finger. Thus, when the index finger is inserted into the pot so that it just touches the top of the rice, the water should cover the top of the rice to the depth of the first joint on the finger, a little less than an inch deep. This gives a personal touch to the cooking of rice.

Bring the water to a fast boil. Stir across the bottom of the pan to be sure the rice is not burning or sticking. Then reduce the flame to the lowest possible level and tightly cover the pot. Do not remove the cover again until the rice is done. If the water begins to boil over, reduce the heat, but do not remove the cover. It takes about 20 minutes from reducing the flame and covering the rice for it to cook. When steam no longer comes out from under the lid, the rice is done. Remove it from the flame and let it sit for another 5 minutes. Then remove the lid, stir the cooked rice well until it becomes light and fluffy, and serve. The other dishes are cooked while the rice is steaming. Thus it should take 25 to 30 minutes to prepare the entire meal.

If watching the stove, waiting for the steam to diminish, and wondering about the cooking process is a bother, an electric rice cooker provides an easy alternative. Wash the rice and cover it inside the electric cooker with the amount of water indicated. There is a two-cup level, a three-cup level, and so forth, indicated inside the rice cooker, so there's no need to worry about how much water to pour into the pot. Electric rice cookers can also be used for stew, soup, and mixed rice-vegetable dishes.

Rice is the usual starch portion of the meal served at a Taoist banquet. However, noodles and bread can sometimes be served as a substitute for rice. Homemade noodles are popular throughout northern China, while packaged noodles of all kinds can be purchased throughout the north and south. Each meal provides starch, protein, and vegetables for a proper balance. One may choose any of a variety of starches to complement the recipes presented here.

Letting Go

Yu, holding on, and Wu, letting go, are related, like
Hard and easy, tall and short, high and low,
Speaking and hearing, before and after.
All of nature
Births and lets go,
Needs no praise for its actions,
Does its work and moves on.
It is because it lets go that it doesn't grow old.

2.

Vegetarian Stew

2 large or 3 medium-sized potatoes
2 medium-sized carrots
*1 large round onion (*yangcun *in Chinese)*
1 small stick of celery
2 soft ripe tomatoes
1 can of mushrooms, if desired

This meal, rich in vegetable protein, can be used alone or as a base for a variety of recipes that follow. Bring 2 cups of water to a boil in a medium-sized pot. Peel and chop the potatoes, carrots, onion, celery, and tomatoes into half-inch or bite-sized squares. Add the mushrooms, if you wish. When the stew is boiling strongly, reduce the heat to a medium flame and add the following:

4 garlic cloves, finely chopped (3 if mild flavor is preferred)
1 teaspoon of cumin
2 tablespoons of mild soy sauce
Juice of half a lemon
1/2 teaspoon of finely chopped lemon peel
1 tablespoon of sugar
1 cup of grape wine (China Red), if desired.
*Sprig of cilantro (*xiangcai*), if desired*

Let this mixture boil until the potatoes and carrots are cooked. The stock can be thickened by adding 2 tablespoons of cornstarch dissolved in 1/2 cup of water, or it can be served as a soup. Add more soy sauce, or salt, if desired. The stew can be served over rice or thickened and poured over noodles. Serve it with a green vegetable, Cucumber and Tomato Salad, fried dofu (bean curd), or other recipes, as you please. The same stock is used for Vegetarian Curry, in the next recipe.

Full Belly

Don't reward the mighty, there'll be no contention;
Don't call things precious, there'll be no thieves.
Don't stare with lust, the heart will be peaceful.
Empty the heart, fill the belly,
Weaken selfish desire, strengthen the bones.
Let go, Tao will rule.

3·

Vegetarian Curry

Vegetarian Curry with rice has become a popular dish in China, Hong Kong, and Taiwan. This recipe allows the same basic ingredients as the Vegetarian Stew, but adds new spices:

2 *large or 3 medium-sized potatoes*
2 *medium-sized carrots*
2 *cloves of garlic, chopped*
1 *large round onion (yangcun)*
2 *soft ripe tomatoes*
1 *small stalk of celery*
1 *can of mushrooms, if desired*
2 *tablespoons of curry powder (Chinese or Japanese style)*
2 *level teaspoons of cumin powder*
1 *teaspoon of cardamom, if desired*
1 *teaspoon of turmeric or saffron*

Follow the directions for recipe 2, Vegetarian Stew, but add curry powder, additional powdered cumin, and cardamom to the soup stock and some turmeric or saffron to give a warm curry color. Serve the curry over rice. Garnish the plate with sunflower seeds, raisins, a tablespoon of a semi-sweet fruit jam (see recipe 57), and plain yogurt, and serve with Cucumber and Tomato Salad (recipe 16).

Tao Is a Bowl

Tao is a bowl full of good things, never used up.
It blunts sharp edges, unties knots.
At ease in the bright lights,
It's at home with the soiled and dusty too.

4.

Many-Bean Stew

One of the most popular dishes in the traditional Taoist health diet is Vegetarian Bean Stew. The cook usually tries to include eight kinds of beans or a combination of beans with other healthy ingredients. Eight is a sacred number in the ancient *Yijing* (*I-ching*, Book of Changes). It represents the cyclical changes that take place in nature, including the four seasons, plus the four directions, the human life cycle, the ideal family (father, mother, three boys, and three girls), and the cycling process to and from the gestating Tao.

A variety of beans and grains are available in the Chinese market. Supermarkets usually carry a prepackaged eight- or fifteen-bean mixture that can be used instead of searching for the individual ingredients. Any variety of beans and grains can be used, according to taste. The following recipe was suggested by a Taoist acupressure healer who practices in Beijing.

1 cup each of red, white, and black beans
1 cup each of green, yellow, and brown lentils
1/2 cup of cornmeal
1/2 cup of millet
1/2 of a white onion, chopped
3 cloves of garlic, chopped
1/2 teaspoon of finely chopped lemon peel
2 tablespoons of brown sugar
3 tablespoons of light soy sauce

Variation: to make the bean stew sweet, add the following:

1/2 cup of peeled, dried lychee,
or
1/2 cup of peeled, dried dragon-eye lungyan *lychee*
1/2 cup of chopped dates

Let the beans soak for about 12 hours. Wash all of the beans carefully before cooking. Be sure there are no small stones in the packages, especially if purchased in a streetside market. Then boil the beans over a medium flame, and lower the heat to a simmer for about 2–3 hours, or until they are somewhat softened. Next add the lentils and all of the other ingredients and let them boil together for another hour. Serve a bowl of this thick and nutritious soup to guests on all auspicious festival days. It is thought to be especially good for the elderly and those who are weak or tired. Add the sweet ingredients on festival days and to assist recuperation.

Look Inside

Heaven and earth don't have favorite things,
Taoist sages don't have favored people.
Treat all like sacred objects.
Look inside to find it.

Dofu (Bean Curd) and Garlic

Dofu (tofu) is a high-protein soybean food that is smooth and easy to digest. It has an almost indistinguishable fine taste of its own and picks up the flavor of the spices and vegetables with which it is cooked. It can be used daily as part of a healthy vegetarian diet. There are four or five kinds of dofu available in most Asian markets. The most common form is the retangular soft white chunk refrigerated just after cooking and sold in sealed packages. It will keep in the refrigerator for two or three days but is best cooked when fresh.

1 package of firm white dofu (14 or 16 ounces)
2 or 3 cloves of garlic
1/2 cup water used to soak dried mushrooms (see recipe 7)
2 or 3 tablespoons of mild soy sauce
1 teaspoon cornstarch
2 tablespoons cooking oil

Take the dofu out of the plastic wrapper and drain off the water. It can be laid on a paper towel to remove excess moisture. Then chop 2 or 3 cloves of garlic, depending on taste, and press the garlic with the flat blade of the knife before chopping into fine pieces. Cut the dofu into small bite-sized squares to cook with the garlic.

Take 1/2 cup of the water used to soak dried mushrooms for another dish (see recipe 7) and mix with the the soy sauce and cornstarch. Keep this aside to pour over the cooked dofu in the hot pan once it is cooked.

Heat a wok or frying pan and add the oil. Put half of the garlic into the hot oil, to flavor it. Then place the dofu squares into the hot pan. The pan will sizzle and the hot oil may splash, so cover the pan immediately with a lid. Turn the heat down to medium and let the dofu brown for about 2 minutes. Then take the lid off and turn the dofu over, so that the other side may brown as well. Throw the rest of the chopped garlic over the dofu at this point and cover again for 2 minutes. This is the basic way of preparing tasty dofu for a vegetarian meal. Serve with a dash of low-salt soy sauce splashed over the surface of the dofu. Or, for a fancier version, pour the mushroom water, soy sauce, and cornstarch mixture over the dofu in the wok and stir as it thickens. This makes an expert restaurant-style dish to serve with dinner.

Mother Spirit

Deep in the valley is a mother spirit who doesn't die,
A mystery woman.
At the doorway of this woman
Is heaven and earth's source.
Forever spinning, never tired, she's always there.

6.

Dofu With Spinach

The dofu cooked in the previous recipe tastes very good when placed over a bed of freshly stir-fried spinach. Buy a bunch of freshly cut spinach from the market. Wash it well and leave the stems in water until ready to use, to maintain its freshness. After the dofu has been removed from the frying pan in recipe 5, take the spinach out of the water and shake it, leaving some drops of water on the leaves. Place the spinach in the hot frying pan and stir it with wooden chopsticks or a spatula so that both sides touch the hot oil still in the bottom of the pan. Then cover the pan and let the spinach simmer for 1 minute. Stir the spinach again, and cover. After 30 seconds or so, check to see how the leaves look. Spinach should not be allowed to overcook. A bright green color should remain in the leaves, and the bright pink ends of the spinach stems should be even brighter.

Take the pan off the stove and put the spinach on a chopping board. Cut the leaves and bottoms into inch-long bite-sized pieces. This can be done without burning the fingers by using a large Chinese-style chopping knife. Then put the spinach on a dish and place the dofu on top of it. The contrast between the green spinach and the lightly browned dofu is particularly appetizing. Sprinkle roasted sesame seeds over the dish for a finishing touch. Splash 3 tablespoons of low-salt soy sauce over the dish before serving.

Always Giving

Heaven and earth are always giving, always birthing.
Why? Because they are not selfish.
That is why they can always be fertile.
The Taoist sage is not selfish, and thus is fertile too.

7.

Dofu, Mushrooms, and Bamboo

Mushrooms and bamboo shoots can be used in a variety of ways with dofu. Dried mushrooms can be purchased in any Asian food market. Japanese *shiitake* mushrooms and Chinese dried mushrooms from Fujian province in southeast China are sold in most supermarkets. Dried mushrooms should be rinsed carefully before they are put to soak. Put them to soak before going to work in the morning, and use them for dinner that night. This dish tastes best when served with rice.

1 bamboo shoot or can of bamboo shoots, cut into thin slices, julienne style
6 or more dried mushrooms, soaked for 4 or more hours, then sliced into quarters
1 package of dofu, about 1 pound, cut into bit-sized squares
Cooking oil
2 or 3 cloves of garlic, chopped
1/2 teaspoon sugar
2 or 3 tablespoons mild soy sauce
1 teaspoon cornstarch
1/2 cup of the mushroom soaking water

Bamboo shoots are a fine source of nourishment and roughage. Canned bamboo shoots are readily available in food markets and can be mixed with most stir-fried dishes. Cut the bamboo shoots lengthwise into thin inch-long slices. Cut the soaked and softened mushrooms into quarters. After frying the dofu as in recipe 5, remove it and set it aside. Add a bit more oil, another teaspoon of chopped garlic, and the sugar, and throw in the mushrooms and bamboo shoots to sauté. Cover the pan and cook for about 3 minutes at medium heat, then remove the lid and stir. Return the fried dofu to the pan and let the mixture simmer for another minute. Mix the soy sauce and cornstarch into the 1/2 cup of mushroom water and pour it into the wok. Stir until the cornstarch thickens. Serve on a plate decorated with a leaf of lettuce or cabbage.

Water Is Best

Water is the best of all. Without contention,
It does good for all things.
It goes to the lowest place, which others avoid.
Because of this it is closest to Tao.

8.

Dofu and Mixed Vegetables, "Family Dofu"

One of the most popular dofu dishes in the vegetarian repertoire is the recipe called Family Dofu (*jiachang dofu*) found on almost every Chinese restaurant menu. It can be made in a variety of ways. Use recipe 7 and add carrots, bell peppers, and other ingredients.

Dofu, mushrooms, bamboo shoots as in recipe 7
1 clove of garlic, chopped
1 medium-sized carrot, cut into thin inch-long strips
Cooking oil
1 tablespoon of fresh ginger root, chopped
1 small can of water chestnuts, chopped into thin slices
1 small, mild green and 1 red bell pepper, if desired
1/2 cup mushroom soaking water
2 tablespoons soy sauce
1 teaspoon cornstarch

After cooking the dofu in the garlic, set it aside and simmer the thinly sliced carrot in the pan for 3 or 4 minutes. Then remove the carrot, reheat the pan, and put in 2 tablespoons of oil. Add the chopped ginger and stir-fry for about 30 seconds. Then reduce the heat to medium and add the bell peppers, if desired, the chopped water chestnuts, carrot, dofu, bamboo shoots, and mushrooms. Let this mixture simmer for 1 or 2 minutes.

Now mix a sauce made of the water the mushrooms soaked in, the soy sauce, and the cornstarch. Pour this mixture over the vegetables and dofu and let it simmer for another 30 seconds, or until the sauce thickens. One may add two or three kinds of mushrooms to this dish, for variety. One may also use deep-fried dofu (found in Asian supermarkets) and garnish the dish with a bit of Chinese parsley (cilantro).

For the simplest dish, use the first four ingredients only: the dofu with the garlic, the mushrooms, bamboo shoots, and carrot. Use the fancier style when guests come.

Heaven's Way

Better stop short than eat too full;
A blade too sharp will soon be dulled,
A house filled with jade and gold will soon be emptied.
Pride in honors and wealth brings misfortune.
When your work is done, let go.
This is heaven's way.

9.

Water Chestnuts and Snow Peas

Water chestnuts are found in the Asian section of most modern markets. Snow peas, which are usually very expensive, make a fine dish when mixed in thrifty quantities with the less expensive water chestnut. The dish can be topped with unsalted cashew nuts, a surprisingly delicious dish for family and guests.

1 small can of water chestnuts
1/2 pound of snow peas
Cooking oil
1 teaspoon garlic, chopped
Light soy sauce
1/4 pound of unsalted cashew nuts

Drain the can of water chestnuts and chop them into thin slices. Wash and destring the Chinese snow peas and cut them in half. Heat the wok or frying pan and put in only 1 tablespoon of oil. Throw in the snow peas and let them sizzle for about a minute, or until they turn a delicious bright green. Lower the heat and add the water chestnuts, letting them simmer for about 1 minute. Throw the chopped garlic into the pan, and 1 or 2 tablespoons of light soy sauce. Serve on a clean plate, with cashew nuts sprinkled over the top.

Keeping It Together

How keep body and mind one?
Be like a child.
Be aware of breathing, be soft and pliant.
To see the transcendent Tao, have a pure mind,
. . . don't say "no."
To receive heaven's blessing,
Be empty like a mother's womb,
Give birth and nurture, then let go.

10.

Water Chestnuts, Snow Peas, and Dofu

This dish is prepared in the same manner as recipe 9, except that dofu is used instead of cashew nuts.

Cooking oil
1 package of dofu (14 to 16 ounces)
3 cloves of garlic, chopped
1/4 pound of Chinese snow peas
1 small can of water chestnuts, finely chopped
2 or 3 tablespoons of mild soy sauce

Heat the wok and add 2 tablespoons of oil. Cut the dofu into 1-inch squares (about 1/4 inch thick) and fry in the oil until both sides are browned. Remove the dofu and set aside for a moment. Put the chopped garlic in the wok, and add the snow peas, then the chopped water chestnuts. Stir-fry briefly, about 1 minute, until the snow peas are a bright green. Then add the dofu and stir for another 30 seconds. Serve steaming hot with rice, green vegetables, and Cucumber and Tomato Salad (recipe 16).

Hollow Center

Thirty spokes on a wheel are useless,
If the center isn't hollow.
A porcelain bowl is worthless, unless empty.
Doors, windows, and inner space
Make a room livable.
Sell possessions to make a profit,
Empty things to make them useful.

11.

Dofu with Peanut Sauce

One of the most popular dressings in south China and Southeast Asia is peanut sauce, known in Thai and Laotian cooking as satay sauce. In this recipe, found while looking for Taoist priests in the Min dialect area of southern Fujian and northern Kwangdong provinces, peanut sauce is used with fried dofu.

The peanut sauce:
2 tablespoons of peanut oil, or other oil
1 clove of garlic, chopped
1/2 cup of water
1 cup of peanut butter (any supermarket peanut butter)
1 cup coconut juice or milk
Juice of 1 lemon or 1 lime
1 teaspoon of brown sugar, if desired
2 tablespoons of soy sauce, to flavor and darken the sauce
1/2 teaspoon of lajiao, *Chinese red pepper, if desired*

The dofu:
3 tablespoons of peanut oil, or other oil, for frying
1 package of dofu (14 to 16 ounces) cut into 1-inch cubes
Chopped cabbage, to cover and garnish a serving plate
1 tomato, sliced into 8 pieces
Thinly sliced lemon
Cilantro or mint leaves

First prepare the peanut sauce. Heat a small pan and put in the 2 tablespoons of oil and the crushed garlic. Then add the water, peanut butter, and coconut juice, and bring to a boil while stirring. Add the lemon or lime juice, brown sugar and soy sauce, and continue stirring. Let the mixture simmer for another 2 or 3 minutes, until it is smooth and thick. A taste of Chinese red pepper, called lajiao, may be added if desired. Set this aside, to be poured over the dofu, tomatoes, and cabbage, when ready.

Heat the wok and put in the 3 tablespoons of oil. Fry the dofu slices until they are brown on both sides. Arrange the finely chopped cabbage on a serving plate, with the 8 slices of tomato around the edges. Put the fried dofu in the center of the plate and pour the peanut sauce over the top. Garnish with thin slices of lemon, and cilantro or mint leaves for color. This recipe should serve 4 people at a banquet.

Meditation XII

Look Within

Color blinds the eye, sound deafens the ear.
Flavor dulls the taste, hunting muddies the heart.
Raising prices makes men thieves.
The Taoist sage fills the belly, not the eyes.
Value what is inside, not what is outside.

12.

Snow Peas, Bamboo, and Mushrooms

Snow peas prepared with bamboo and mushrooms make a good accompaniment to Dofu with Peanut Sauce (recipe 11). Use a bit of sugar in this dish as a variation to the garlic-flavored recipes.

2 tablespoons of cooking oil
1/2 cup of sliced bamboo shoots
1/2 pound of Chinese snow peas
4 dried mushrooms, soaked for 30 minutes
1 small can of straw mushrooms, or button mushrooms
1/2 cup of mushroom soaking water
1 teaspoon of cornstarch
1 teaspoon of light soy sauce
1/2 teaspoon of sugar, if desired

Heat the wok and put in the cooking oil. Put in the bamboo shoots, then the snow peas, and fry for about 2 minutes at medium heat. Cut the soaked mushrooms into thin strips and add them to the wok, along with the straw mushrooms, or button mushrooms if desired. Let the mixture simmer for another 2 minutes or so. Take a 1/2 cup of the mushroom water and mix in the cornstarch and light soy sauce. Pour this mixture into the wok, giving a fine shiny appearance to the dish, and serve hot. This dish is a favorite at the Yuanxuan Xueyuan Taoist vegetarian restaurant.

Run From Praise

Be happy when scolded,
Fearful when praised.
By the very fact that this body is alive,
Difficulties and contradictions come to us.
If we were dead, disasters wouldn't occur.
So value difficulties, if you value your life.
Only when we forget selfish interests
Can we be entrusted with ruling the world.

13.

Eggplant and Soybean Paste

One of the easiest to use and tastiest ingredients in vegetarian cooking is soybean paste. It is made from cooked and slightly fermented soybeans that are mashed and preserved in flavoring and a little salt. The Japanese name for this paste is *miso*. It can be bought in the Asian food section of most supermarkets, either in its Chinese (soybean paste) or Japanese (miso) version. In this recipe it is made into a sauce and poured over eggplant as it fries in a wok.

2 long eggplants, or 1 round eggplant
3 tablespoons of cooking oil
3 cloves of garlic, finely chopped
1 cup of water
1/2 cup of miso, soybean paste

Cut the eggplant into bite-sized chunks. Heat the wok and put in the cooking oil. Throw in the chunks of cut eggplant and stir-fry at medium heat for about 3 minutes. Throw the chopped garlic into the wok and add 1/2 cup of the water. Let this simmer for 2 to 3 minutes while mixing the miso paste with the remaining 1/2 cup of water. Pour the water and miso mixture into the wok, and cover. Let this simmer for another 4 to 5 minutes, or until the eggplant has absorbed the miso flavor. Serve hot with steamed rice. Do not let the miso burn on the bottom of the pan. Add a little more water if necessary.

Fried dofu can be added to this dish as a special variation. For those who like hot pepper, add a teaspoon of lajiao, Chinese red pepper sauce.

Swimming in Tao

Can't see it, hear it, or touch it,
The transcendent Tao.
Jump into it, swim in it.
Not too shiny on the surface,
Not too dark inside. . . .
Can't see it in front of me,
Can't catch up from behind.
From the reality of now,
We know old Tao's footprints.

14.

Spinach, Soybean Paste, and Sesame

Soybean paste can be made into a wonderful sauce or marinade to be used in a number of recipes. The following dish uses spinach as a base to mix with a soybean and sesame seed sauce. Make enough of this sauce to be used as a dip in other recipes.

1 pound of fresh spinach
1/2 cup roasted sesame seeds, ground into a paste
1/2 cup of soybean paste (miso)
1/4 cup of light sweet wine, or 1 teaspoon of sugar
1 tablespoon of light vinegar
2 tablespoons of cooking oil

Wash the spinach thoroughly and place whole with roots attached in a pan of water to keep it fresh until ready to cook. (The spinach roots are a tasty part of this dish.)

Heat the wok but do not put any oil into it. Pour the sesame seeds into the heated wok or frying pan, and stir until they are roasted to a light brown but not burned. Put the fragrant roast sesame seeds into a blender, or grind them with a pestle for about 2 or 3 minutes, until the oil in the seeds is released. Mix the soybean paste, the sweet wine (or the teaspoon of sugar), and the light vinegar into the sesame paste. Continue to stir until it becomes a smooth paste. Add a little water if necessary, to make it into a dip.

Reheat the wok and put in the oil. After 30 seconds or so, put the spinach into the wok and stir-fry for about 2 minutes. Remove the wok from the flames and put the spinach onto a cutting board. Chop the spinach into inch-long bite-sized lengths and put it into a bowl. Then pour some of the dip over the spinach. Mix the dip and the spinach together so that the freshly cooked leaves are coated with the dip. Serve this dish as an accompaniment to freshly cooked rice and a dofu recipe.

Uncarved Wood

Long ago Taoists took goodness as their master,
Touched the subtle, wondrous mysteries of Tao . . .
Such as shivering when wading in a winter creek,
Careful not to disturb the neighbors,
Polite and thoughtful when invited as a guest,
Sensitive as ice beginning to melt,
Simple as an uncarved block of wood,
Unspoiled as a wild valley meadow,
Cleared of mud and silt like a placid pond.
One can only keep this kind of Tao
By not getting too full,
Stay new and fresh like sprouting grass.

15.

Soybean Paste and Cucumber

One of the easiest cold dishes to serve with any meal is cucumber cut into bite-sized pieces, with a dressing. In this recipe cucumber is served either with soybean sauce as a dip, or with the soybean-sesame mix in recipe 14.

- 2 *Asian cucumbers, well washed and sliced*
- 1 *cup of soybean paste (miso), or*
- 1 *cup of soybean paste-sesame seed dip (see recipe 14)*

The thin, long Asian cucumber has less acid and is easier to digest than the smooth-skinned Western variety used to make pickles. Either kind of cucumber will do for this recipe, but the Asian variety is easier to cut and prepare.

Great care must be taken in washing fresh vegetables bought in open markets in China. First wash the vegetable with detergent, then pour boiling water over it to remove any bacteria from fields where night soil is used, as it is in most of Asia. In Western kitchens, it is not necessary to use detergent and boiling water, although careful washing is always a good idea because of pesticides.

If a Western cucumber is used, slice it in half and quarters and remove the seeds in the center, then slice the cucumber into bite-sized pieces that can be picked up with the fingers and dipped into the soybean paste. Put the cucumbers on a plate, with the cup of soybean paste (or the soybean paste/sesame seed dip) in the center. Replenish the sauce as necessary.

Inner Peace

To achieve inner peace, be completely empty.
All things around us are busily working,
Watch them, returning to Tao.
Have eyes only for finding your roots.
Peace is found in returning to Tao.

16.

Cucumber and Tomato Salad

A tasty cold dish that is found widely throughout the monasteries and vegetarian restaurants of China and Southeast Asia is Cucumber and Tomato Salad. It can be served with any of the hot dishes above, either as an appetizer or with the main meal.

2 Asian cucumbers
1 tomato
1/2 of a sweet onion, red or white
3 tablespoons of rice vinegar (or light balsamic vinegar)
2 tablespoons of water
1 teaspoon of sugar

Cut the cucumbers into thin slices. Cut the tomato into small square pieces. Finally, chop the onion half into small pieces and mix well with the tomato and cucumbers. Put the vegetables into a bowl and prepare the sauce. Mix the rice vinegar, water, and sugar in a cup until the sugar is dissolved. Pour the mixture into the bowl and mix with the cucumber mixture. More or less vinegar can be used according to taste. This recipe serves 2 or 3 people. It is best eaten immediately and not stored. Seconds can easily be made on request.

The Best Boss

The best boss is scarcely seen or known.
The next-best boss is loved.
The third-best boss is feared.
The worst boss is hated.
If the boss can't be trusted,
The workers will be unfaithful too.
The best boss seldom speaks. When the job is done,
The workers say, "We did it!"

Bean Sprouts and Dofu

Bean sprouts are a good source of vegetable protein and can be bought in most modern supermarkets. They can be prepared alone, with dofu, or with a variety of vegetables.

1 pound of bean sprouts
3 tablespoons of cooking oil
1 14-ounce package of dofu cut into 1-inch cubes
1 teaspoon of sugar, if desired
2 or 3 tablespoons of light soy sauce
1 cup of water
1 teaspoon of sesame oil

Wash the bean sprouts well and let them drain. Heat the wok, add 2 tablespoons of the oil, and brown the dofu on both sides. Remove the dofu and add the remaining tablespoon of oil to the wok. Put the bean sprouts into the wok and stir-fry for about 2 minutes. Dissolve the sugar in the soy sauce and pour this over the bean sprouts. Now add the fried dofu to the mixture, and the cup of water. Cover the mixture and let it simmer for about 6 or 8 minutes, stirring occasionally. When almost done, pour in the sesame oil, stir once more, and serve hot.

How Tao Disappears

When Tao disappears, "benevolence" and "justice" emerge.
When "wisdom" and "pundits" come, so does deceit.
When family love is lost, everyone talks about
Filial piety and compassion.
When the country is without law and order,
Politicians appear.

18.

Bean Sprouts and Vegetables

Bean sprouts can be prepared with a variety of vegetables, following recipe 17. Lunch in a monastery always includes a bean sprout dish of some sort. The ingredients, once cooked, can also be wrapped in a "spring roll" tortilla (thin-rolled and pan-fried bread) and deep-fried.

1 long or 2 short carrots
1 small stalk of celery
2 tablespoons cooking oil
1/2 teaspoon of chopped ginger root
6 dried mushrooms soaked for an hour, finely chopped
1 small can of mushrooms (optional)
1/2 can of chopped water chestnuts (optional)
1 pound of bean sprouts
1 cup of the mushroom soaking water
2 or 3 tablespoons of light soy sauce

Chop the carrot into fine strips about an inch long. Chop the celery into small pieces. Heat the wok and add the oil and chopped ginger, then stir-fry the carrot and celery for about 2 minutes. Next add the mushrooms and water chestnuts, if desired, and stir for another minute. Finally, add the bean sprouts and simmer for about 30 seconds. Pour in the cup of water in which the mushrooms were soaking, cover the wok, and let the contents simmer for about 5 or 6 minutes. Splash the finished dish with 3 tablespoons of light soy sauce and serve hot.

Embrace the Simple

Get rid of saints and sages,
Everyone will benefit.
Do away with "benevolence" and "reciprocity,"
Family love and compassion will return.
No more "good deals" or "big profits,"
Thieves will disappear.
All of the above lack a simple rule!
Get rid of selfish desire, embrace the simple Tao.

19.

Dofu, Celery, and Carrots

The basic ingredients in recipe 18 can be combined with thin strips of hardened dofu instead of bean sprouts. Buy the hardened form of dofu in a Chinese market, or cut fried dofu into thin inch-long strips.

1 14-ounce package of hard dofu
1 large or 2 small carrots
1 stalk of celery
2 tablespoons of cooking oil
Dried mushrooms, soaked for an hour
1/2 teaspoon of chopped ginger root (or dried powdered ginger)
1/2 cup of mushroom soaking water
2 tablespoons of light soy sauce
1 teaspoon sugar (optional)
1 tablespoon of cornstarch

Cut the dofu, carrot, and celery into inch-long thin strips. Heat the wok and add the oil, then the chopped ginger. First stir-fry the carrot and celery strips for about 2 to 3 minutes, then add the dofu and mushrooms. Let this simmer for about 3 minutes. Meanwhile, mix the mushroom water, soy sauce, and sugar together with the cornstarch until it is smooth, with no lumps. Pour this mixture over the ingredients in the wok, and let them simmer until the sauce thickens. Serve hot with rice and green vegetables.

Nature's Table

No more "erudites"! Do not "fear"
The difference between "Eeh" and "Ooh"
Or what's good and bad for me.
Need I fear what others fear? Such nonsense.
Happiness is to possess nothing.
Be uncontained as the ocean, free as the wind,
Eating at mother nature's table.

Zucchini, Carrots, and Celery

The same ingredients used in recipes 18 and 19 can be used with zucchini or mild light squash (butter, green, winter squash). The vegetables are steamed together instead of fried, for those who prefer to avoid oil.

1 pound of zucchini or other light squash
1 carrot
1 stalk of celery
2 or 3 cloves of garlic, crushed
3 or 4 dried mushrooms, soaked in 1 1/2 cups water for an hour
2 to 3 tablespoons of light soy sauce, if desired

Chop the zucchini into small pieces. Chop the carrot and celery into thin strips. Put all of these ingredients into a pot and cover them with the water in which the mushrooms soaked. Bring to a boil and then simmer over a moderate burner for about 15 minutes (do not overcook). Add the garlic and the mushrooms, and boil for another 2 or 3 minutes. There should be very little moisture left when done. Sprinkle with the soy sauce and serve.

What Is Tao?

"Only follow the Tao!"
"But what is Tao?"
"It is hoo-hoo, gwang-gwang,
Or is it hoo-gwang, gwang-hoo?
It's a form, a thing,
It's dark, it's 'bright,'
Wise, true, faithful. . . ."
"How do you know?"
"Here inside me!"

Winter Squash

One of the most popular kinds of squash in vegetarian cooking is the winter squash, which may be used in soups as well as in fried and steamed dishes. The winter squash is quite large, light in color, and can be bought in the markets in smaller half or quarter sizes.

1-pound slice of winter squash
1/2 can of bamboo shoots
2 to 3 tablespoons of cooking oil
2 cloves of garlic, crushed
1/2 teaspoon of sugar, if desired
1 cup of bamboo shoot water
1 teaspoon of cornstarch
1/2 cup of water
2 tablespoons of soy sauce

Cut off the skin and remove the seeds of the winter squash. Cut the squash itself into triangular pieces about 1 inch long and 1/2 inch wide. Chop the bamboo shoots into thin inch-long strips, saving the water in which the bamboo shoots came. Heat the wok, add the oil, and stir-fry the squash for about 2 to 3 minutes. Add the bamboo shoots, garlic, and sugar, if desired. Finally, pour in the 1 cup of bamboo shoot water. Let the dish simmer over medium heat for about 4 to 5 minutes. When the squash appears translucent the dish is done. Thicken the sauce by mixing the cornstarch in the 1/2 cup of water with the soy sauce, and pour it into the wok for the last 30 seconds or so of cooking.

Bend to Be Whole

Bend to be whole, curl up to be straight.
Be empty to be filled, old to become new.
Owning little brings peace;
Owning much brings confusion.
Embrace Tao, be patterned by nature.

22.

Potatoes

Potatoes of all sorts, taro root, sweet potatoes, and mountain yams are popular throughout China. They are prepared in a number of ways, including the stews described in recipes 2 and 3. Sweet potatoes are roasted in streetside stalls and can be purchased to be eaten during an evening walk. Regular white potatoes (called *tudou*, "earth beans," or *malingshu*, "horse-bell potatoes") are served as a vegetable dish rather than as a starch. They can be peeled and cut into bite-sized pieces to be fried in the wok, or cut into fine three-inch threads to be cooked al dente with a little vinegar.

3 medium-sized potatoes, peeled and washed
3 to 4 tablespoons of cooking oil
1/2 teaspoon of salt
1 teaspoon of sugar

Cut the potatoes into triangular wedges about 3 inches long and less than 1/2 inch wide at the base. Heat the wok and put in 3 tablespoons of the oil. When the oil is hot, add the salt to keep the oil from splashing, then put in the potatoes. Cover and fry over medium heat for about 5 minutes, stirring so that the bottoms do not burn. Then add a little oil down the side of the wok, turn the potatoes over so they fry on the other side, and cover for another 5 minutes or so, or until the centers are soft. Add a little sugar toward the end of the process, which will darken the color and seal in the flavor. Serve hot, with Cucumber and Tomato Salad, and one of the dofu dishes. This recipe was learned from Lin Na, a young law professor at Guilin (Kuei-lin) University, who is an excellent cook and ballroom dancer.

Violent Winds

Violent winds last only a morning,
A great rainfall is over in a day.
Heaven and earth make sure . . .
Violence does not endure.

23.

Fried Potato Strings

Another tasty potato dish found on most vegetarian menus is called *tudou* or "fried potato strings." To make this dish properly the potatoes must be cut into very thin long strips and fried in a hot wok until they are barely done (still slightly firm). The potato strips should still be white and fresh when served.

3 tablespoons of cooking oil
1/2 teaspoon of fresh chopped ginger root
3 medium-sized potatoes, washed and cut into very thin strips
1 tablespoon of mild vinegar or balsamic vinegar
1/2 teaspoon of chopped red pepper, if desired

Heat the wok and add the oil and chopped ginger. When the oil begins to smoke, put in the potato strings and stir them vigorously so that all sides are coated with the hot oil but the potatoes themselves do not turn brown. Add the vinegar and, if desired, the red hot pepper. Serve immediately.

On Tiptoe

Don't stand on tiptoe too long,
Don't try to walk far on your knees.
A show-off has no glory,
A self-seeker has no fame. . . .
Leftover food, burdensome deeds,
Tao is not there.

24.

Stir-Fried Cabbage Strings

Prepare this dish in the same manner as recipe 23. Thinly sliced cabbage is sautéed briefly and served freshly cooked from the wok. Wang Jing learned this dish from her mother, who is from the Islamic city of Yinquan (Yin-ch'üan) in the province of Ningxia (Ning-hsia) on the Silk Road.

1 medium-sized cabbage, finely shredded
1/2 teaspoon of shredded ginger root or ginger powder
3 tablespoons of cooking oil
3 teaspoons of balsamic or light white vinegar
1 teaspoon of salt

Wash the cabbage and shred it into long, thinly sliced strings. Chop up a small slice of fresh ginger (or use ginger powder) and measure 1/2 teaspoon to be used in the wok.

Heat the wok and pour in the oil and the salt. When the oil is hot (so that a drop of water bounces from it), add the chopped ginger and stir. Next, throw in the chopped cabbage and stir for about 1 minute, so that each strand touches the hot oil. Then pour in the vinegar, cover the wok with a lid, and reduce the heat to medium. Let the cabbage mixture simmer for about 3 minutes, stirring occasionally so that it doesn't burn. Serve hot with any of the dofu, bean, or stew dishes in the preceding recipes.

Nature's Mother

Born from chaos, before heaven and earth, . . .
Nature's mother is called taiji, *(*t'ai-chi*),*
Tao breathing inside me.
Man, earth, and heaven follow Tao breathing
inside me.
Taiji *follows* wuji, *Tao that is of itself.*

Cabbage, Mushrooms, and Chinese Pepper

Baicai (*pai-ts'ai*) or napa cabbage is one of the staple foods of north China during winter. The cabbage is harvested in large quantities during October and November. Tons of the freshly harvested heads are carried daily into the city to be stored outside the house or in cold corridors during winter. The outer part spoils and then freezes, protecting the inner core throughout the cold winter. Many people survived on this vegetable alone during the Cultural Revolution. The leaf is a crunchy smooth white at the roots, growing upward into a tall triangle and turning into a curly green. The following recipe comes from Ho Minjie, an artist who uses Taoist art symbols as a motif for weaving tapestry.

*1 teaspoon of crushed Chinese peppercorn (*huajiao*)*
5 leaves and stems from 1 medium-sized napa cabbage
5 dried mushrooms, soaked in water for an hour
3 tablespoons of cooking oil
1/2 teaspoon of salt
1/2 cup of mushroom soaking water
Soy sauce (optional)

Crush the Chinese peppercorns with a pestle or in a blender. Wash the cabbage leaves and lay them one on top of another on a chopping board. Cut the cabbage into pieces lengthwise, approximately 3 inches wide, so that the white stem and green leaf are together. When the mushrooms are soft, remove them from the water, saving about 1/2 cup of the water for simmering. (For an artistic effect, you can cut 4 very thin slices from the top of each mushroom, so that a white star appears through the dark surface.)

Heat the wok and put in the oil. When it is hot, just as it begins to smoke, add the salt to keep the oil from splashing. Put in the mushrooms and stir-fry so that both sides are coated in oil. Then let them simmer for 2 or 3 minutes on each side, until they are cooked and the oil is flavored. Remove the mushrooms and set them aside.

Add the cabbage to the wok and stir-fry vigorously for about 1 minute. Then reduce the heat, pour in the reserved mushroom water, and simmer for about 3 minutes. When the cabbage is tender but still fresh and firm, remove from the heat and put it on a plate. Arrange the mushrooms on top of the cabbage, and serve warm. Mild soy sauce can be provided separately for guests who prefer a saltier flavor.

Rooted In Peace

The light of heart are rooted in peace,
The master of motion is always calm.
Rootless, we become light-headed;
Restless, we can't keep Tao's inner peace.

26.

Stir-Fried Napa Cabbage Stems

A surprisingly easy and delicious dish, this recipe comes from the Taoist cook in the restaurant atop Mao Shan. It is made simply from the hard white central part of napa cabbage. It can be fried and served with peanuts, cashew nuts, or mushrooms, or served alone as a side dish to a stew or dofu banquet.

5 leaves from a medium-sized napa cabbage
2 tablespoons of cooking oil
1/2 teaspoon of salt
1/2 teaspoon of freshly chopped ginger root

Variations:
1/2 cup of peanuts or
1/2 cup of cashew nuts or
1/2 cup of fresh mushrooms

Wash the cabbage leaves and cut off the green curly edges, so that the long, triangular, smooth white stem is left. (Save the green part of the leaves for garnish or to use in fried-noodle dishes.) Cut the white part of the cabbage crosswise into 3-inch strips and then cut each strip lengthwise into thin shoestring slices, julienne style.

Heat the wok and put in the oil. When the oil is warm but not smoking, throw in the salt and then the ginger. The salt may be omitted for those on a low- or non-salt diet. If using nuts, add 1/2 cup of peanuts or the 1/2 cup of cashew nuts into the wok.

Stir for about 30 seconds, then throw in the sliced white cabbage stems. Continue to stir-fry for about 2 minutes, not letting the cabbage burn. If desired, add the mushrooms, then turn the heat down to medium, letting the mixture simmer for another minute. Remove from the heat and serve the cabbage stems on a plate garnished with the green part of the cabbage.

Goodness Leaves No Footprints

Good deeds leave no traces,
Good words leave no target,
Good accounting needs no ledger,
Well-locked needs no key or bolt.
Well-tied needs neither rope nor knot.
The Taoist sage helps all, turns none away,
Tao's wondrous way.

27.

Cabbage, Bamboo Shoots, and Mushrooms

For this standard vegetarian dish, any kind of cabbage, Western, napa, mustard, or Cantonese bok choy, can be used. The entire cabbage leaf and the bamboo shoots are first fried together, and then the mushrooms are added. Chopped ginger root is used instead of garlic for flavor.

- *1 cup of dried mushrooms, soaked until soft (all day is best)*
- *1 small head of cabbage, about 1 pound*
- *3 tablespoons of cooking oil*
- *1 teaspoon of finely chopped fresh ginger root*
- *1 medium-sized bamboo shoot, chopped into thin slices or a small can of sliced shoots*
- *1 cup of fresh mushrooms, if desired*
- *1/2 cup of the water used to soak the mushrooms*

Wash the dried mushrooms well before soaking. Wash the cabbage or other greens and cut into bite-sized pieces. Heat the wok and put in the oil. First stir-fry the ginger for about 30 seconds, then put in the bamboo shoots, and then the cabbage. Stir-fry for about 2 minutes. Finally, add the mushrooms, both dried and fresh, if used, and the 1/2 cup of mushroom water, and simmer at medium heat for about 2 minutes. Stir occasionally so that the cabbage does not burn. Serve warm with rice. The mushroom water adds special flavor to the dish. It can be thickened by adding 1/4 cup of water mixed with well-dissolved cornstarch about 30 seconds before removing the wok from the stove, adding a glistening restaurant quality.

New Baby

Know the masculine, preserve the feminine
Become nature's valley, receptive.
Return to being a newborn child.
To go back to Wuji, the transcendent Tao,
Be totally simple.

Green Bell Peppers and Mushrooms

The Chinese green bell pepper is milder than the larger Western variety found in supermarkets, and much easier to digest. Peppers can be prepared in a variety of ways, either with the various dofu (bean curd) dishes in the previous recipes or with noodles as in the following recipes. One of the ways that bell peppers are prepared in China and Japan is simply to charcoal broil them and then pour mild soy sauce over the dish when serving.

One of the most delicious ways of serving the roasted bell pepper is with mushrooms, or in combination with mushrooms and onions.

5 medium-sized green bell peppers
5 dried mushrooms, soaked until soft
1 cup of chopped bamboo shoots, if desired
1 sweet round onion (yangcun)
3 garlic cloves, or
1 teaspoon of chopped ginger root, if desired
3 tablespoons of cooking oil
1/2 cup of mushroom soaking water

Wash and halve the bell peppers, removing the seeds and stems. Wash the dried mushrooms well and set them to soak before going to work in the morning, or soak them overnight to make a strong mushroom stock. Chop the bamboo shoots if used, and the onion into bite-sized pieces. Mince the garlic (or ginger, for a change; use one or the other for flavor).

Heat the wok and put in the oil. When it's hot, add the garlic or the ginger (not both) and stir for about 30 seconds. Add the bell peppers, bamboo, and onion, and stir-fry for 2 minutes. Then add the mushrooms and stir-fry for another minute. Finally, pour 1/2 cup of the mushroom water into the wok, cover, and simmer for about 2 minutes. Remove the bell pepper mixture from the heat and serve hot.

Variations on this recipe: put a teaspoon of ground Chinese peppercorn (huajiao) into the oil with the garlic; splash three tablespoons of light soy sauce over the dish before serving; or add fried dofu, and for a Szechuan taste, add a teaspoon of lajiao (Chinese red pepper) paste.

The World Is Sacred

The world is a sacred vessel,
Not to be tampered with.
Try to control it,
You'll lose it.

29.

Fried and Simmered Squash

There are many kinds of yellow squash in Asian markets similar in taste and style of cooking to the hubbard squash, acorn squash, and pumpkin of the West. One of the most widely used vegetarian methods of cooking squash is to first fry it, then simmer it in a wok with onions, pepper, soy sauce, and a little sugar. This recipe was found in a Taiwanese temple during a Taoist Jiao rite of renewal.

1 hubbard squash (Jpn., kabocha*), cut into 3-inch-square pieces*
3 tablespoons of cooking oil
1 teaspoon of ground huajiao, Chinese peppercorn
1 medium-sized round white onion, finely chopped
1 tablespoon of brown sugar

Wash the squash, cut it into 3-inch-square pieces, and boil it for about 20 minutes in a medium-sized pot of water. Remove the squash and let it cool. Then cut off the tough green skin and mash the squash into a lumpy mush.

Heat the wok and put in the oil. Add the Chinese pepper and the finely chopped onion and stir-fry until it is slightly browned, about 2 minutes. Then pour in the mashed squash and the sugar. Turn the heat down to medium, cover the wok, and let the squash simmer for about 10 minutes. Stir frequently so the squash does not burn or stick to the bottom of the pan.

Serve the cooked squash on a large plate garnished with parsley. Save about half of the cooked squash for the next recipe.

Nonviolence

Use Tao to advise the mighty.
Don't use weapons to conquer the world,
Weapons wound their users.
Where armies camp, weeds thrive.
Where armies march, crops fail.
Better harvest the crops.
Don't use violence, preserve Tao.

30.

Sweet-Sour Vegetarian Fish

Many vegetarian dishes imitate the shape of cooked meat and fish. Though the flavor is different, the final dish looks like baked or fried fish, duck, chicken, or pork. Here are two ways to make vegetarian fish that I leaned in the Yuanxuan Taoist kitchen.

Boil 3 yams or sweet potatoes, or reserve about 2 pounds of yellow squash from the previous recipe. Mash the boiled potatoes and fry them with chopped onion and a little black pepper, as in the previous recipe.

Set aside the cooked squash or sweet potato in the refrigerator until it is cool and firm. Then mold the sweet potato or squash paste into the shape of a fish lying on its side. Make 2 or 3 molded fish, each 5- to 6-inches long.

Heat a flat frying pan and put in about 1/2 cup of oil, enough to fry the vegetarian "fish." The oil should be at about 375 degrees Fahrenheit, to fry the fish quickly. Brown one side, then the other. Then put the fish on a paper towel to drain any extra oil.

Next, make the Sweet-Sour Sauce.

Sweet-Sour Sauce:
2 tablespoons of brown sugar
1/4 cup of sweet white wine
1 tablespoon of cornstarch
1/4 cup of water
2 tablespoons of white vinegar
2 tablespoons of ketchup
1 small can of crushed pineapple in heavy syrup

Mix the above ingredients together in a medium-sized pan, first dissolving the sugar in the wine and mixing the cornstarch into the water. Put the pan over a medium flame and cook the mixture until the sauce thickens.

Arrange the "fish" on a bed of carefully washed fresh lettuce and pour the Sweet-Sour Sauce over it. Serve steaming hot, garnished with parsley. For a variation, include finely cut strips of carrot in the sauce, for color.

Make Peace, Not War

Victory at war is not beautiful.
It is the same as celebrating a funeral.
The man who loves war should not reign.
A Taoist ruler chooses peace and quiet.

31.

Pre-dinner Snacks and Appetizers

When invited to dinner in a Chinese family, always bring along a gift of fruit, crackers, candies, wine, or something edible. The host, in turn, provides plates of peanuts, freshly boiled soybeans in the pod (Jpn., *edamame*), dried fruits of all kinds, and crackers. Some sort of wine or beer is always served at banquets. Since many Chinese do not drink alcohol in any form, soft drinks, tea, and juices are also served to all guests.

Dried fruit—dates, raisins, dried peaches, apricots, apples, and bananas—fresh and roasted peanuts, candied fruits and nuts of all sorts, sweet cookies and crackers, are offered to guests before and after a banquet.

They should be put out in bowls for guests on all occasions. Here is a suggestion for a well-rounded pre- or post-dinner offering:

1 bowl of dried dates
1 bowl of roasted, candied walnuts
1 bowl of mixed nuts (peanuts, pine nuts, cashews, almonds)
1 bowl of raisins
1 bowl of mixed candied fruit

Dried and candied fruit has a special meaning in the Taoist temple and monastic tradition. Since dried fruit keeps almost indefinitely, it is used as a symbol for longevity, good health, and life after death.

In Taoist temples, dried fruits are always offered to guests, with the wish for health and prosperity to those who partake of them. The sound of the word for dried dates is symbolic. *Zaozi* (*tsao-tzu*) means quickly giving birth to a healthy child for the newlywed and early prosperity for a new business. Five kinds of dried fruit and nuts are offered to guests during the Chinese New Year festival, as a blessing for the coming year.

The best place to buy dried fruit in Beijing and other large cities in

China is at a Hui Islamic market. The Hui ethnic group, who legend says are descendants or converts of Tang dynasty (618–907) Muslim traders, maintain special shops and restaurants throughout China noted for cleanliness and quality produce. Dates from the Silk Road, Gansu, and Ningxia provinces, and raisins from Ürümqi, Turfan, and Kashi in Chinese Turkestan (Xinjiang Province) are noted for their flavor.

Nameless

Tao stays nameless,
Tiny in its simplicity.
All nature respects it.

32.

Cakes, Crackers, and Peas-In-The-Pod

Cakes made with baking powder or baking soda, and dry crackers are brought as gifts to a banquet, to be served before and after meals. Freshly baked yeast breads in the Uighur Silk Road tradition are sold in streetside stalls in China; they make excellent pre-dinner snacks, served with beer or soft drinks as appetizers. Here is a suggestion for three kinds of cakes, crackers, and boiled soybeans to be served before a vegetarian meal:

1 bowl of mixed dried salted crackers (Jpn., arare*)*
1 bowl of boiled green soybeans in the pod (Jpn., edamame*)*
1 plate of soft candies made from sesame seeds or peanuts and puffed rice

A bowl of freshly boiled and chilled green soybeans in the pod is often served to accompany drinks from Japan and Korea throughout most of China and Southeast Asia. The dish is easy to prepare. Simply boil fresh soybeans, or peas-in-the-pod, with 1/2 teaspoon of salt in the water, until tender. Drain, cool, and serve in the pod. The guests push the beans out of the pod when eating. Place a bowl on the table for the discarded pods.

A bowl of sweet candies made from molasses and sesame seeds, or puffed rice, peanuts, and ginger, is also set out before most banquets and for guests who come for tea. These sweets can be bought in almost all markets.

Unshelled boiled peanuts and sunflower and melon seeds to be cracked between the teeth are served year-round, on all occasions.

Enough

The wise know others,
The enlightened know themselves.
Violence conquers others,
Strength conquers self.
To know "enough" is a blessing.
Longevity comes after death.

33·

Fresh Fruit

Though Chinese do not serve sweet desserts in the Western fashion, fresh fruit is always a requisite ending to a good banquet. I recommend serving five fruits, in the Taoist tradition.

One large platter of fresh fruit could include:

5 apples
5 tangerines or oranges
5 bananas
A bunch of grapes, in season
Fresh apricots, peaches, or other fruit when in season

Tangerines (*juzi* [*chü-tzu*]) are served after meals from late November through winter and spring. They are a requisite gift at Chinese New Year and bear the symbolic meaning of blessing from heaven (the sound for "heaven," *tian*, and "sweet," *tian*, are the same). Apples have the symbolic meaning of peace (the word for "apple," *pingguo*, sounds like "peaceful crossing"). Bananas represent an open hand praying for peace and blessing. Fresh pears, *li*, are homonyms for *li*, "turning a profit in business." Apricots and peaches in summer are symbols of health and longevity. The Taoist patron of long life, Shouxing, is seen in art and sculpture as a smiling elder carrying a peach in his hand. The serving of fruit after a Taoist banquet is therefore a prayer for the happiness and well-being of the guests.

In China candied mountain apples (haw fruit), small red-skinned crab apples served on wooden skewers, are popular through autumn, winter, and spring. Semi-sweet mountain-apple jelly is sometimes served with meals. Mountain-apple jelly goes well with breakfast cereals and bread.

Tao Is "Home"

Tao is like floodwaters, everywhere.
All creatures depend on it for life,
And none are turned away.
Tao nourishes all, but doesn't boss.
Tao is not selfish, gives a home to all.

Baked Uighur Bread

One of the most popular breads sold throughout North China, and in the larger cities where Uighurs from Xinjiang are present, is the baked *nang*, a circular pizzalike flat bread baked in a charcoal oven. The Uighurs, one of the largest ethnic minorities in China, come from Xinjiang Province, the far northwest of the People's Republic of China. Resembling Mediterranean folk more than Asians, Uighurs live in what was once the ancient lands of the Silk Road, alongside Bactria, Sogdian, Tokharia, and other desert kingdoms. The inhabitants of Tashkent and Samarkand on the former Soviet side of the border also speak this ancient Altaic-Turkish language.

The Uighurs were once devout Buddhists. Kublai Khan stationed Turkish Islamic troops in Xinjiang during the Mongol rule (1281–1365 in China). Buddhism was systematically destroyed and Islam put in its place. Uighurs, Kazakhs, Tajiks (Iranian ancestry), Tatars, and Uzbeks all converted to Islam. The foods of the Silk Road remained the same, however, as did the wine. Though Uighurs are devoutly Muslim in belief and abstain from pork and shellfish, they still drink the sweet red and white desert wines grown along the Silk Road.

Uighur nang is baked like pizza and other Mediterranean breads. The flour is mixed with yeast, allowed to rise twice, kneaded, and rolled into flat dough. Before baking, dried onion flakes can be mixed in the dough. The freshly baked bread can be bought in the streets of Beijing in the early evening and served with beer or soft drinks before meals.

No Harm

Tao attracts all creatures to itself,
And never harms anything.
It gives peace, great happiness,
And food for passing guests . . .
Never used up.

35.

Uighur Noodles

Vegetarian Uighur noodles are sold throughout north China, along the Silk Road from Gansu, Province to Xinjiang. A delicious meal can be prepared in minutes, using this simple formula. One can make homemade noodles or buy ready-made pasta in a supermarket.

The following recipe comes from Turfan, along the old Silk Road in the Taklimakan Desert, Xinjiang. Next to the city are remains of a fifth- to sixth-century Buddhist city, its adobe walls crumbling in the desert winds and heat. Below the ruins in a fertile oasis is the modern city of Turfan, a sleepy hamlet that is a whistle-stop for foreign tourists coming to enjoy the grape festival in August. Turfan is famous for its sixteenth-century mosque, its sweet wine and fresh melons, and its dried green raisins sold throughout China. After visiting the ancient ruins and the mosque in 120-degree heat (Fahrenheit), our party stopped at a small Uighur restaurant for a vegetarian banquet. The following noodles and sauce dish was served.

3 green bell peppers
3 ripe tomatoes
1 large white onion
3 tablespoons of cooking oil
1/4 pound of string beans
4 cloves of garlic, chopped
1 tablespoon of fresh cumin seed, from the Turfan market

Chop the peppers, tomatoes, and onion into bite-sized pieces. Heat the wok, put in the oil, and stir-fry the onion, tomatoes, and bell peppers for about 2 minutes. Reduce the flame and let them simmer. Cut the string beans into 1-inch lengths and put them into the simmering wok, along with the freshly chopped garlic. Let simmer for another 2 minutes, until the vegetables are tender but still fresh. Pour this mixture over noodles that have just been boiled and sprinkle the dish with the cumin.

Some like this dish served hot, with a dash of lajiao, red Sichuan pepper, added. It is also served as a meat dish, with small pieces of barbecued lamb shish kebab mixed in with the sauce.

Weak Overcomes Strong

Cloth must be stretched before shrinking,
Weakness follows great exertion.
What is thrown down must first be lifted up!
Great talent wears out.
Thus, weakness overcomes strength.
Leave fish in the water,
Weapons in the sheath.

Homemade Noodles

The Uighurs and Islamic Hui restaurants that serve the previous dish also make their own noodles. I learned the following recipe from Buniya, a Uighur ballad singer from the music and dance department of the Academy of Ethnology in Beijing.

1 pound of white flour
1 cup of boiled, and then cooled, water
1 teaspoon of salt
2 tablespoons of cooking oil

Put a large pot of water or a large wok half filled with water on the stove to boil. While waiting for the water to heat up and boil vigorously, prepare the noodles from dough prepared as follows.

Pour flour out on a large wooden chopping board that has been scrubbed clean and dried. Make a depression in the center of the flour, as in the top of a volcano. Pour a few tablespoons of the boiled and cooled water into the flour and begin working it into a ball of evenly mixed dough. Use more or less of the water (depending on the dampness or dryness, cold or heat of the weather) until the flour has been mixed into a smooth ball of dough.

Knead the dough with the ball of the hands, as when making bread, for about 8 to 10 minutes. Then cut the rounded ball of kneaded dough into halves, then quarters, and eighths. Take the small balls and roll them out into pasta sticks about a foot in length and an inch thick. Rub your hands with oil and roll out one of the sticks until it is about 1/4 inch thick and 3 feet long. Drape this long piece of rolled dough over your shoulders (place a towel over your neck and shoulders to keep the long thick noodle clean).

Now step up to the pot of boiling water, and pull off small diagonal slices about 1/2 inch long and drop them into the boiling water, by pressing the dough between thumb and index finger. Some cooks slice off the end of the long noodle by using a dull knife. Cut enough thin-pressed thumb-length noodle slices into the boiling pot to make 2 or 3 plates of noodles, and then cook the fresh pasta for about 8 to 10 minutes, or until they are al dente. Drain the noodles and pour them onto 2 or 3 plates. Cover the noodles with the tomato, onion, and bell pepper sauce made in recipe 35. Sprinkle a tablespoon of fresh cumin seeds or cumin powder on top.

Tao Makes No Fuss

Tao doesn't make a fuss, and gets things done.
If only politicians were able to do this,
All would be well by itself.
When things get out of control,
Simplicity sets all straight.
When desires are extinguished,
Nature calms us down.

Tomato, Onion, and Bell Pepper Stew

One of the healthiest dishes found from Gansu Province across the Silk Road into central Asia is a stew made of the same ingredients used on Uighur noodles. Instead of being fried, the vegetables are boiled.

2 onions
4 tomatoes
3 bell peppers
1 cup of boiling water
1/2 teaspoon of salt
4 garlic cloves, chopped
1 teaspoon of cumin, if desired

Cut the onions, tomatoes, and bell peppers into bite-sized pieces. Put a cup of water into a pot, add salt, and bring to a quick boil. Put in the onions, tomatoes, and bell peppers and let them cook for about 5 minutes. Add the garlic, reduce to medium heat, and let cook for another 10 minutes, until a thick vegetable stew is made. Put a teaspoon of cumin into the soup before serving. Noodles may be added, or the soup can be used as a dip for nang, pizza bread.

It is said that people who eat this stew regularly become immune to the common cold. When the stew is served with noodles, Uighur restaurants add bite-sized chunks of roast lamb for flavor.

Eat Fruit, Not Flowers

When Tao is lost, virtue takes over.
When virtue is lost, goodness follows.
When goodness goes, obligation rules.
These are the husks, not the kernel.
Eat the fruit, not the flowers.

38.

Mongolian Hot Pot

When traveling in the high grasslands of Inner Mongolia, it is impossible to avoid eating roast or boiled lamb, at least as a condiment to the soup in which vegetables are cooked. Mongolian Hot Pot is one of the most famous dishes in the Mongolian shaman tradition. A shaman is a healer and priest or priestess of the ancient Mongol religion. Though Buryat Mongol shamans were suppressed in the former Soviet Union, as were shamans in Mongolia proper, a small group of shamans still practice in the far northeast of Inner (Chinese) Mongolia. It was from a Mongolian shaman that I learned the following recipe.

1 pound of baicai, napa cabbage
1 bunch of long green onions or scallions
1 pound of lean lamb meat
1 bunch of chopped cilantro
1 14-ounce piece of dofu, chopped into half-inch squares
1/2 pound of translucent bean noodles (Jpn., harusame*)*
2 cups of bean paste–sesame seed sauce (recipe 14)
5 whole pickled garlics for appetizers

The Mongol shaman brought to the feast a piece of lean young lamb meat given to him in payment for a healing service. He put pieces of chopped cabbage and chopped green onion stems into a pot of water boiling over a charcoal fire, and then added thin slices of the lamb. Cilantro was added for flavor.

After cooking the meat and vegetables for a while, the shaman added pieces of dofu and translucent noodles to the boiling water. He placed a rice bowl with 2 or 3 tablespoons of soybean and sesame seed sauce before each of the four guests. The guests chose cooked pieces of meat, vegetable, dofu, and noodles from the pot with chopsticks. Each piece was first dipped in the soybean and sesame sauce, and then eaten.

Quantities of beer and pickled garlic slices were consumed with the banquet. Loaves of oven-roasted bread, and fermented mare's milk were also served to the guests. The Taoist tradition allows for the eating of a few pieces of lamb in this instance, to show appreciation for the feelings and customs of the host.

One With Tao

Because they are one with Tao,
Heaven is clear, earth at peace,
The soul is spiritual, the valley is fertile,
Nature gives birth, rulers are pure and simple.

39·

Pickled Vegetables—Lunch in a Kazakh Yurt

A part of the province of Xinjiang (Chinese Turkestan) bordering on Kazakhstan in the former Soviet Union is the home of the Kazakh sheep and cattle herders. The Kazakhs were pastoral nomads, living in a rounded mobile tent-like structure called a yurt. Rather than a conical tent, the Kazakh yurt is made by bending bamboo slats into a large inverted basket, over which canvas or skins are stretched for protection from the desert winds and freezing winter snow. The walls inside of the yurt are decorated with colorful woolen blankets and woven Oriental rugs.

Cooking in the yurt is done over a small charcoal stove, with the chimney or smoke ascending through a small hole in the center of the ceiling. The hole in the roof was thought to be the gateway to heaven, through which the shaman traveled in former days to find healing spirits.

Today the Kazakhs are for the most part Islamic, subsisting mainly on lamb, wheat-and-barley bread, buttered tea (see recipe 42), and some vegetables. When you are traveling through the Taklimakan or Gobi Desert or the high grasslands where Kazakhs tend their sheep and cattle, it is easy to get invited for lunch in a nomad's yurt.

Roast lamb on a skewer, the boiled and seasoned stomach and intestines of the lamb, yogurt, a large loaf of baked bread, and pickled or preserved vegetables and garlic are served to visitors. To make pickled vegetables, place fresh, cleaned vegetables in a one-quart jar with a tightly-fitting lid. Add 1/4 cup of uniodized salt. Add water to cover, and close the jar. Let it stand overnight. The longer you let it sit, the stronger the flavor will become.

For the vegetarian, yogurt, vegetables, buttered tea, and baked bread are an energy-filled diet for living in the extremes of desert heat and winter cold. A stew made of vegetables, lean lamb meat, and homemade noodles is served at night.

Tao Returns

Returning is Tao's movement.
Yielding makes Tao useful.

40.

Tibetan Barley Bread—Lunch in a Tibetan Temple

Tibetan Buddhist temples can be found in Gansu, Sichuan, Yunnan, and the high mountainous province of Qinghai in northeast Tibet. Travelers who wish to visit Lhasa may choose to go through Chengdu in Sichuan or take an express train to Xining City in Qinghai, and from there ride trains and buses over the nineteen-thousand-foot pass from Lake Kokonor southward into Tibet, a much longer but more authentically Tibetan experience.

Qinghai is the birthplace of many famous Tibetan monks. Tsong Khapa, founder of Yellow Hat Gelugpa Buddhism, was born there, as was the present Dalai Lama.

My host at the monastery was the abbot of the fine arts college, one of the five sections of a Tibetan temple. After a tour of the temple grounds and sacred art collections, we were invited by the abbot for lunch. The chief disciple of the abbot, a young man in his late teens from a nearby Tibetan farming family, prepared a meal of Tibetan bread made from roast barley flour; fresh dri yogurt (dri is the term for a female yak; yak is the word for a bull, thus it is improper to say "yak's milk," even in such a miraculous place as Tibet); tsampa, a roll made of butter, tea, and roast gingke barley flour; vegetables fried with a little roast lamb for flavor; and Tibetan tea.

The recipe for Tibetan barley bread follows the general formula for baking bread elsewhere. One-half cup of roasted barley flour is used for every two cups of wheat flour. To this is added a little millet flour, for flavor. When kneading the bread, the monks mix in crushed sesame and sunflower seeds for flavor, coating the surface of the bread with soft dri butter. The flavored ingredients are rolled and kneaded, making an artistic pattern when the freshly roasted bread is broken and eaten for lunch.

Tao Is Hidden

The best pottery is the last from the kiln,
The best music makes no sound,
Great art has no form.
Tao stays hidden, without fame.
Yet only Tao's work endures.

41.

Dri Yogurt

The Kumbun temple (Taer Si) is a popular place of pilgrimage. Birthplace of Tsong Khapa, founder of the Yellow Hat Gelugpa sect, the temple has become a source of revenue for the state-run Religious Affairs Bureau, which charges admission fees to the pilgrims and tourists who enter each of its many grand temples. Street merchants sell silk scarves called *khata* (pronounced "hata"), bricks of Hunan dark tea, and bowls of freshly made yogurt. So fresh is the yogurt that drops of melted yellow butter sometimes appear on the surface, separated from the rich cream drawn off to make dri butter.

Yogurt is a popular form of high-protein food that is sold throughout China. There is certainly no more delicious form than that made from the milk of the dri. Streetside stalls and vendors offer it to the tourists and pilgrims who visit this important religious shrine. The yogurt is eaten straight from the bowl or mixed with a bit of brown sugar for easier digestion.

The vendors' silk scarves and blocks of Hunan brick tea make excellent gifts. The khata silk scarves come in white, bright yellow, and blue silk. Bright yellow is the proper color to give to an abbot. Khata are given on all festive occasions in Tibet, such as when going to or leaving a friend's home, at a banquet, in thanks for receiving a favor, at a wedding, or to welcome a guest. One should buy a khata and a brick of tea before visiting a famous abbot.

One, Two, Three

Tao births One (life breath).
One births Two (male yang).
Two births Three (female yin).
Three give birth to all things.
This is because One, Two, and Three are in harmony.

Buttered Tea in a Tibetan Monastery

At the suggestion of the abbot of the monastery art college, we purchased a yellow khata and a kilo of fine Hunan brick tea and walked through the temple grounds toward the monastery of Buddhist learning. The famous Buddhist monk Kejia Rimpoche teaches here. We were ushered into his room, bowed with the abbot of the art college and the younger monks, and listened to Kejia Rimpoche talk of tantric Buddhist meditation.

While he was speaking, a younger Tibetan Buddhist made tea in the following way:

1 large pot of boiling water, about 1 gallon
1 cup of tea leaves broken from the hard brick of dark tea
1/2 pound of dri or other butter
2 tablespoons of salt
2 tablespoons of sugar, if desired
3 cups of dri or other milk

Let the tea leaves boil for about 10 minutes, until the tea is quite dark and strong. Then pour the tea into a churn, much like a churn used to make butter. Pour the butter, with milk, salt, and sugar into the tea, and churn vigorously for about 5 minutes, or until the tea and butter are thoroughly amalgamated. If there is no churn handy, lower the heat and stir the simmering butter and tea vigorously and continuously for about 5 to 8 minutes.

Pour the tea into bowls such as are used to eat rice. Serve freshly baked barley bread with the tea, with sesame seed candy or some other sweet.

Since Hunan brick tea is not readily available in most Western supermarkets, any black tea may be used instead. For those who cannot use salt, a bit of sugar may be used in its place. Buttered tea is surprisingly delicious and gives a strong burst of energy for walking at the fourteen thousand- to sixteen thousand- feet heights of northeast Tibet.

Meditation XLIII

Tao Lets Go

When "hold on" and "let go" enter a space,
"Let go" benefits.
"Let go" is Tao's way,
Taught without words.
All nature learns it.

43.

Tsampa: Roast Barley Meal with Tea and Butter

One of the staple diets of the Tibetan plateau is *tsampa.* Made of roast barley flour and dri butter mixed with tea, this energy-laden freshly rolled cereal provides enough energy to survive in a healthy and sturdy physical condition in the Tibetan highlands. Since the dri does not flourish below twelve thousand feet the making of authentic tsampa is limited to Tibet.

Tsampa is offered by the monks to guests at all meals. It is especially important to eat tsampa for breakfast, in order to have the energy for the great amount of walking and climbing required to get to Tibetan monasteries.

One cup of roast gingke barley flour per person
1/2 bowl of strong Tibetan tea
1/4 cup of dri butter per person
1/2 teaspoon of salt (omit if the tea is already salted)
1/2 teaspoon of sugar

Take the 1/2 bowl of buttered tea and gradually mix in the roast gingke barley flour until a smooth thick paste, not unlike a ball of dough, has been kneaded. Work the dough a bit with your fingers, adding enough flour to make it firm but not dry to the taste. Give a roll of the tsampa to each of the guests. Tsampa is eaten with Tibetan tea, baked barley bread, and yogurt. Though a high-fat diet can cause heart trouble, high cholesterol, and other problems at sea level, the energies needed to survive in the Tibetan highlands seem to render harmless the effects of dri butter on the body's circulatory system.

Though the flavor of roast gingke barley and dri butter is difficult to match, this recipe can be duplicated using black tea, butter, and some other whole grain flour, cream of wheat, or instant oatmeal. Perhaps the high mountains are the ideal place to try it.

Meditation XLIV

Know When to Stop

The body is more important than fame,
The body is more important than wealth!
"Profit and loss" are ailments,
"Madly in love" is misfortune . . .
Know when to stop, you'll live longer.

44.

Tea Served To Guests

It is a strict custom, observed throughout China, to serve tea to guests. The serving of tea represents a sign of welcome, and tea is a refreshing drink in the heat of summer or cold of winter. A variety of teas, far more than in the average Western supermarket, are available in specialized tea shops.

Brick tea, which can be purchased in small, medium, and large blocks, comes from the province of Hunan in southwest central China. This tea has been a favorite of Tibet, Xinjiang (Chinese Turkestan), and most of the Silk Road areas for more than a millennium.

In the United States special teas can be found in Asian markets, and in larger cities you will find specialized tea shops that carry a great variety of Chinese teas.

The Tibetan manner of preparing brick tea was described in recipe 42. Steeped brick tea is also served in Uighur restaurants and homes without any other ingredients added. The tea has a milder taste than strong black tea from India. It is served to guests and with meals in the Uighur household.

Mongol and Kazakh herdsmen serve brick tea with mare's or goat's milk and a little sugar. The cold winds of the Mongolian steppes pierce through even the warmest clothes. Brewed brick tea provides the best protection against chilblains and hypothermia in wintry weather.

Pure And Peaceful

The greatest success leaves a little undone.
Fill almost full, leave a little room.
The straightest bends slightly,
The smartest looks dumb,
The best argument is silence,
Move a little, don't freeze!
Be still, don't perspire!
The pure and peaceful rule nature.

Tea With Chrysanthemums

The province of Yunnan in southwest China is famous for a smaller rounded form of brick tea called *pu'er cha* (*p'u-erh ch'a*). When bought in a package in hard unbroken form it is called *pu'er tuocha* (*p'u-erh t'uo-ch'a*). It can be purchased in most Chinatown markets, such as those found in San Francisco, New York, Los Angeles, and Honolulu. This form of brick tea is best for hot climates. It provides a cooling effect for guests who come on a hot sultry day.

The Cantonese and many Hong Kong businesses serve this tea with dried chrysanthemum blossoms, an exquisite gourmet drink. Mr. Zhao Zhendong provides this tea to guests at the Yuanxuan Xueyuan in Kowloon.

Small dried yellow chrysanthemums about the size of buttons can also be served with a meal. Bring about 2 cups of water to a boil and add a cup of dried chrysanthemum flowers. Wait until the water comes to a boil, then reduce the heat and let the petals simmer for about two minutes.

Strain out the water, put the chrysanthemums on a plate garnished with a bit of fresh lettuce, and flavor them with a tablespoon of light soy sauce.

Enough Is Plenty

When the world has Tao,
Horses are valued for their droppings.
When the world loses Tao,
Horses are used for war.
Not to know when to stop
Is the greatest calamity.
Know what's enough, there'll always be plenty.

46.

Gongfu Tea

The word *kung fu,* seen in so many martial arts books and TV movies, is pronounced *gongfu* in modern Chinese. The word here means "leisure," or meditative breathing, rather than martial arts or self-defense. It also refers to a way of making a thick, gourmet form of *wulong (öolung)* tea in the provinces of southeast China.

This kind of tea is served in Taoist households throughout south Fujian and northeast Guangdong. It is made in a small teapot and served in very small cups, about the size used to serve heated rice wine (sake). Gongfu tea is meant to be enjoyed in a quiet, unhurried environment. One must have gongfu free time, to serve and enjoy it.

The quality of the wulong tea used to make gongfu cha is high—the tea sells for more than a hundred dollars a pound. The first leaves cut in spring are used, and the drying process is carefully supervised. The tea must be used soon after buying. The flavor is quickly lost by exposure to air, so it is kept in an airtight container. To make gongfu tea, the following utensils are required:

1 large metal pot for continuously boiling water
1 small ceramic teapot (brown Yixing ware is preferred)
5 small matching teacups
1 ceramic tray

Boil a pot of water and pour it over the teapot and teacups arranged on the tray. Let the water fill the teapot and the cups, overflowing onto the tray. Then pour the hot water out of the cups and the pot and put about 4 tablespoons of wulong tea in the pot, filling it one-half to two-thirds full, according to the strength of the tea desired. Pour boiling water over the tea leaves, and immediately pour the water out. The boiling water on this first round is simply used to purify and wet the leaves. It is not meant to be tasted or drunk.

Now pour boiling water over the leaves a second time, and cover the pot with a tightly-fitting lid. Pour more boiling water over the closed teapot. Let it sit for 3 or 4 minutes, then pour the tea into the tiny cups for the guests to drink. The fragrance of the tea should be appreciated, before drinking.

Stay Home

No need to leave one's door,
To know the whole world.
No need to squint out the window,
To see the Tao of heaven.
The farther you travel, the less you know.
The Taoist knows without going,
Sees without looking, succeeds without doing.

47.

Mao Shan Green Tea

The leaves of green tea grown around the base of the Taoist mountain Mao Shan are among the tastiest in China. Visitors to the monastery are served with cups of this light, refreshing summer drink while they discuss meditation and the beauties of the view from the summit.

To brew this tea, only the purest of water should be used, preferably from a well or from rainwater caught from the temple roof. It is said that during the Tang and Song dynasties emperors were served this green tea made with dew collected from the needles of the pine trees growing on the slopes.

Green tea, it is thought, is the best drink to take after a Chinese banquet. The amount of oil and greasy meats served at the Chinese banquet are frequently difficult to digest, or are hard on the body. The drinking of green tea counteracts the effects of oil and grease on the digestive system.

The tea is sold by the kilo at the foot of Mao Shan, but it is also available in blue canisters about eight inches tall, and three inches in diameter in Beijing and other large city tea shops.

Act Like Tao

Act like Tao, nothing will be undone.
To win the whole world, first give it up.

48.

Dragon Well Tea, "Jade Dew"

Another form of expensive gourmet tea is *longjing* (Dragon Well) tea which is grown in the area of Hangzhou, in central China. These long, thin tea leaves are grown in the shade, then hand-wrapped and dried so that the bright green color is retained.

Dragon Well tea is served when the weather is warm and sultry. It keeps the guest cool even on the hottest days of summer. It can be quite expensive, sometimes four to five dollars an ounce. Serving this tea to guests is a sign of respect and welcome.

Light green teas of central China and Japan can be served in a manner that is known as Jade Dew (Jpn., *gyoku-ro*). To make this kind of tea, be sure that the leaves are quite fresh and clean.

Jade Dew tea is made in the same fashion as gongfu tea, except the water is allowed to cool to 110 degrees Fahrenheit before it is poured over the leaves. Bring the purest of water to a boil, and then let it cool until it no longer burns to the touch.

Measure out 2 teaspoons of the tea leaves into a small teapot. The brown earthenware from Yixing in Jiangsu Province is preferred, because it preserves the flavor. Yixing pottery is made from clay scraped off the bottom of the Yixing River. It is kept in a heated kiln until it turns a brownish purple color. Since the flavor of the tea stays in the pot, one teapot is dedicated to making each kind of tea in the Taoist guest room.

Let the tea steep for exactly 1 minute and 30 seconds, and then pour it into tiny cups. This tea's fragrance should also be enjoyed before drinking.

Tea is always made a second time from the tea leaves. Many say that the second brew tastes better than the first. It is often slightly bitter on the second pouring, so the guest is offered sesame candy or a cookie between cups. After the second brew, throw out the leaves and start over.

Kind To Everyone

The real Taoist is good
To the kind and unkind.
True to the faithful and unfaithful.
Because Tao is good and kind to all . . .
Smiling on everyone.

49.

Ginger Root and Ginseng Tea

Many people cannot drink regular tea, black or green, because of the caffeine content or other reasons. A variety of herbal teas can be served to guests from ingredients found in the Chinese market. Ginger root, fresh or powdered, makes an excellent tea for cold wintry days. It can restore energy after a hard day's labor.

Put a 1/2 teaspoon of powdered ginger or finely chopped fresh ginger in the bottom of a teacup. Fill the cup with freshly boiled water and then mix in 1 teaspoon of honey. The amount of ginger can be varied according to preference for mild or strong taste.

Ginseng is another form of health tea taken to restore energy and vitality when tired. Powdered ginseng comes in little packets, to be dissolved in a cup of boiling water. Chinese doctors recommend using ginseng frequently when tired or recovering from illness. A little ginger powder and honey added to the ginseng tea makes a very palatable drink.

Live Well

A person filled with goodness
Meets no lions or rhinos on the road,
Is untouched on the battlefield,
Is no target for the bull's horns,
No catch for the tiger's claws,
No aim for the soldier's sword.
Why not? Goodness is unscathed by death.

50.

Black Tea With Cinnamon and Lemon

The following drink was served to me in the home of Aniwar, a young Uighur artist from Ürümqi in Xinjiang, in northwest China. Both Chinese and Tibetan guests find the mixture pleasing. Black teas from India or from Yunnan can all be used in this formula. For this tea use a porcelain teapot (not Yixing ware, or other ceramics).

2 quarts of boiling water
2 tablespoons of black tea
1 lemon, cut into 8 slices
2 teaspoons of honey, or 1 teaspoon of sugar
1/4 teaspoon of cinnamon
1/4 teaspoon of freshly ground cardamom, if desired

Pour some of the boiling water into the teapot and teacups to warm them before using. Then put the 2 tablespoons of black tea into the teapot and pour in about a quart of boiling water. Let the tea sit for at least 3 minutes but less than 5 minutes, for the best flavor.

Fill a teacup about 3/4 full, and then squeeze in the juice of one lemon wedge. Add about 1/2 to 1 teaspoon of honey, to taste, and sprinkle a little cinnamon on top. Stir well. Freshly ground cardamom can also be sprinkled on top, if desired.

This formula soothes the common cold, sore throats, and children's discomfort. If a second pot of tea is desired, add a tablespoon of fresh tea leaves over the used leaves, and fill again with boiling water. The teacups are kept filled with tea, as bowls are kept filled with nuts and dried fruit, while guests are present.

Nature Mother Nourishes

All things worship Tao and respect nature mother
Spontaneously. Why? Tao first gives birth, then
Nature mother nurtures, raises, teaches,
Shelters, nests, feeds, renews us,
And stays hidden.

51.

Breakfast Rice

Breakfast is an important meal for those who combine hard work with meditation. The monastic Taoist high in the hills chants morning, noon, and evening prayers, grows vegetables in mountainside gardens, performs various kinds of physical and meditative exercise, and walks up and down the hills surrounding the monastery. The Taoist who works in the city performs rites of blessing for the living, healing for the ill, and burial for the dead. Eating good food regularly, especially in the morning, is important for a happy and healthy life. Taoists usually eat a bowl of softly cooked rice (called *zhou* in mandarin, *chuk* in Cantonese) for breakfast. The rice (often leftover from the night before) is boiled until the cooked grains "open up like flowers" (*hua kaile*), that is, they become large, soft, and easy to digest. This soft rice is served with a variety of condiments, including roasted peanuts, dates, figs or other dried fruit, steamed vegetables, deep-fried bread sticks (*yutiao*), and a highly nourishing soup made from sweetened peanut and soybean paste (*doujiang*).

It is important to eat slowly, especially at breakfast. This is because the stomach can receive only so much well-chewed food for each swallow. Otherwise, quickly swallowed food is said to get stuck in the esophagus, causing bad breath and indigestion. The Taoist is taught to "go to bed when the sky darkens, arise with the first light of dawn," allowing plenty of time for the morning meditation, exercise, and breakfast.

Nature Mother's Children

Everything under heaven has a beginning;
It is nature mother. . . .
From the children, know the mother.
They go back, hold on to her,
Fear no harm.

52.

Oatmeal for Breakfast

Besides the highland barley and butter cereal called tsampa, freshly rolled oat flakes (*yanmai pian*) are also available in many local markets. Oatmeal is thought to be good for children and effective as an agent for cleaning excess oil and fat from the blood.

1 pot of black tea, enough for 3 full cups
1 teaspoon of sugar, as desired
1/2 cup of milk or 1/2 cup of plain yogurt
1 cup of cooked oatmeal
1/2 cup of raisins
2 tablespoons of chopped walnuts or almonds
1/4 teaspoon of cinnamon

Oatmeal is easy to prepare. Make a pot of black tea and pour a cup of this into a bowl. Mix a little sugar and milk, or plain yogurt, into the hot tea, and then pour in the hot oatmeal. To this add some dried raisins, chopped walnuts or almonds, and a dash of cinnamon. Stir well and eat while hot. Drink the rest of the tea with your breakfast.

Tao's Path

If I knew as much as a tiny seed
Growing on Great Tao's path,
I'd only fear losing it.

53.

Oatmeal Bread

Freshly baked quick-rising cakes and breads are sold each morning in the streetside stalls of Beijing and other cities of China. The shops in front of Taoist city temples sell a variety of hot breakfasts to pilgrims and visitors. The same sort of quick-rising breads can be baked at home, early in the morning. Prepare the batter shortly after arising, then put it to bake. After washing and meditating, take the oatmeal, corn, or other bread out of the oven and enjoy a warm breakfast.

3/4 cup of rolled oats
1 cup of flour
2 tablespoons of sugar
1 teaspoon of baking powder
1/2 cup of raisins or chopped dates
1/2 cup of chopped walnuts
1 cup (more or less) of warm milk tea
cooking oil

Preheat your oven to 375°F upon arising. Mix the oatmeal, flour, sugar, and baking soda in a small bowl. Then add the dried fruit, nuts, and liquid, and stir just enough to wet all of the ingredients. Pour a little cooking oil into in a 8 x 4 x 2 inch metal pan and spread it evenly on all the surfaces of the pan. Pour in the batter and bake for 20 to 25 minutes at medium high heat, 375°F, or until done. Put a chopstick into the cake to see if the center is done. The cold dry weather of winter in north China requires more liquid, while the hot humid weather of the south requires much less, for a well-textured bread. Some of the cake can be taken to work as a snack during the day. Serve with homemade fruit jam.

Body Knows Nature

The body understands the body,
The family looks after the family,
Villagers provide for the village,
The country protects its land,
Nature regulates nature.
How do I know about nature?
From my own body.

54.

Dried Fruit and Nut Bread

One of the popular breads sold in morning markets is a quick-rising loaf made with dried fruit, nuts, and a yellow cake batter. Eggs are not used when the bread is made for the Taoist diet. The bread keeps well and can be used on journeys and for a snack with tea when guests come. The packages of multicolored dried fruit and a mixture of nuts can be bought in Islamic markets.

1 cup of white flour
3/4 cup of barley or other dark flour
1/2 cup of sugar
1/2 cup of chopped nuts (walnuts, cashews, almonds)
1/2 cup of chopped dried fruit
1/2 cup of cooking oil or butter, as desired
3/4 cup of tea and warm milk mixed with 1 teaspoon of baking powder or *3/4 cup of yogurt and tea mixed with 1 teaspoon of baking soda*

Mix the dry ingredients together in a bowl. Add the nuts and dried fruit, and then wet the mixture with the cooking oil or butter and milk-tea or yogurt-tea. Use enough liquid to make a thick batter, but do not mix too long. Pour into a small pan, and bake for 20 to 25 minutes at medium-high heat 375°F. Fruit and nut bread goes well with tea.

The Newborn Child

Be peaceful like a newborn child.
Bees won't sting,
Serpents won't bite,
Beasts won't maul,
Birds won't claw.
Though its bones and tendons are soft,
Its tiny fingers hold fast.
No hang-ups on sex, no energy lost,
It cries all day and never gets hoarse.

55.

Cornmeal Bread

Cornmeal bread can be made in the same way as in the previous baked bread recipes, or fried in a tightly covered pan. Most markets carry a variety of ground grain flour. In Chinese markets, the shopper can often choose cornmeal from open bags of grain according to the desired texture and color. Choose a bright yellow cornmeal for making this morning corn bread.

2/3 cup of cornmeal
3/4 cup of flour
1 teaspoon of baking powder
1/2 teaspoon of salt, if desired
1 cup of milk-tea
3 tablespoons of cooking oil (or butter)

Mix the dry materials in a bowl. Then stir in the warm milk-tea and oil until the flour mixture is just dampened. Since the milk-tea is warm, the batter will begin to rise immediately. Pour the batter into a greased 8 x 4 x 2 inch pan and let it bake at 350°F about 20 to 25 minutes, or until done. Cornmeal bread can be served with vegetable stews and curry as well as at breakfast.

Meditation LVI

Speechless

Those who know Tao don't speak,
Those who speak don't know Tao.

Corn Bread with Fruit

One can mix various kinds of fruit with the cornmeal batter and bake them together for a variation at breakfast. Use a recipe similar to the previous one, but put fresh fruit such as apricots, peaches, or apples on top of the bread, just before baking. The flour will rise over the fruit as it bakes. Sprinkle a tablespoon of sugar over the fruit, if desired, to make it sweeter. Cinnamon may be sprinkled on the apples.

2 cups of flour
1 cup of cornmeal
1/2 teaspoon of salt, if desired
1/2 cup of cooking oil
2 cups of warm milk-tea mixed with 3 teaspoons of baking powder or *2 cups of yogurt-tea mixed with 1 teaspoon of baking soda*

Mix the dry ingredients together, then add the oil and mix out the lumps. Add the liquid, mixing just enough to wet the batter. More or less moisture must be used according to the time of year and the weather. During dry winters you will require a little more liquid. Pour batter into an 8 x 4 x 2 inch pan and bake for 25 minutes at 375°F or until the top of the cake is brown.

Presidential Advice

Have no desires,
The people will live a simple life.

57·

Fresh Fruit Jam

Fruit is seasonal in China and is sold in open streetside markets. It is usually brought as a gift to a host's family or a Taoist monastery when one is invited to a meal. Since guests bring an overabundance of fruit, which tends to spoil easily in hot weather, the fruit can be made into a fresh jam and kept for a few days longer. This recipe is not meant for canning. It should be used within a week of making. The secret of the taste and texture of the mixture is the use of lemon juice and a bit of finely chopped lemon peel. The fruit should be fresh and not quite ripe for the best flavor. Use more lemon juice if the fruit is overripe.

1 pound of peaches, apples, or apricots
1 cup of boiling water
Juice of half a lemon
1/2 teaspoon of finely chopped lemon peel
1/2 cup of sugar
1/4 teaspoon cinnamon, if apples are used

Peel and slice the peaches or the apples, but slice and leave the skin on the apricots. Put the fruit into the boiling water and add the lemon juice and the finely chopped lemon peel. Bring the water to a strong boil and add the sugar. Stir until the sugar dissolves, and then turn down the heat. Let the mixture simmer for about 30 minutes, or until the fruit is slightly glazed. Add 1/4 teaspoon of cinnamon to the apple jam.

Fresh fruit jam can be eaten with toast, cereal, or corn bread for breakfast and served as a condiment to accompany vegetable curry. Add a red plum to the boiling fruit to give the jam a bright reddish hue.

A Taoist Sage

Square without sharp edges,
Sculptured but not overpolished,
Straight but not uptight,
Bright but not dazzling,
Such is the Taoist sage.

58.

Open Fruit Pie

Another popular sweet dish brought by guests to a banquet is a pastry shell fruit pie. Pastry shell pie is sold in most bread and sweet shops in north China. It is an excellent dessert to serve after a vegetarian meal that delights Russian, Chinese, Uighur, Kazakh, and other Silk Road palates. The fresh fruit jam made in recipe 57 can be used to cover the baked pastry, or an open pie can be made from scratch.

The pastry:
2 cups of white flour
1/2 teaspoon of salt, if desired
3/4 cup of vegetable oil or butter
1 tablespoon of ice water

The filling:
Fresh fruit jam, or
1 pound of peeled, sliced apples, or
1 small jar of strawberry or other store-bought jam

Mix together the flour and oil (or butter) until a dough that is easy to roll on a board is formed. Use more or less flour, depending on the weather and the wetness of the dough. Mix in the tablespoon of ice-cold water and knead the dough until firm. Sprinkle flour on a very clean wood chopping board and roll out 2/3 of the pastry into a circle that will fit into a small oven (about an 8-inch diameter). Lay the pastry on a flat pan and put the fresh fruit, the fresh fruit jam, or the contents of the jar of jam into the center of the pastry and turn up the edges so that the fruit does not spill over the side when baking. Roll out the remaining 1/3 of dough and cut it into strips. Lay these over the top of the fruit, for an artistic effect. If using apples for the filling, sprinkle 1/2 teaspoon of cinnamon and 1 tablespoon of sugar over the top. Bake on a flat pan for about 25 minutes at 375°F, or until the pastry shell is brown.

It is difficult to say how hot to keep the oven during baking, since electricity is quite erratic throughout most of China. The stove in my Beijing apartment maintains a temperature of about 375°F. If a Chinese oven is used over a gas or charcoal flame, raise the stove or baking pot off the fire with a brick on each side of the flames. Keep a close eye on the baking process, so that the shell does not burn.

Always Caring

Those who follow mother Tao's way live long . . .
Deep roots, firm branches.
Mother Tao is always birthing,
Always caring.

59.

Steamed Cornmeal

The electric rice cooker or a simple pot of boiling water provides an easy way to prepare a healthy breakfast. This recipe can be used with oatmeal, barley, and other brown flours, as well as corn. Seedless raisins or dried dates can be used for flavoring.

2 cups of boiling water
2 cups of cornmeal
1 cup of raisins, or
1 cup of chopped dates
1 tablespoon of sugar
1/2 teaspoon of salt, if desired

Bring the water to a boil and stir in the cornmeal, so that it does not form lumps. When the mixture is smooth, bring it to a boil again, and add the raisins or dates, sugar, and the salt (although it is best to leave the salt out).

Turn the heat down very low and let the porridge simmer, much as when cooking rice. The porridge will turn into a thick, moist cake in about 15 to 20 minutes. Remove it from the heat, and turn it out onto a plate. Use a knife to cut it into slices or a spoon to serve it in a bowl. Fresh fruit jam can be put over the top, or it can be eaten without other condiments. Serve guests cups of hot black tea flavored with cinnamon and lemon.

Small Fish

Ruling a great nation is like cooking a small fish.
When Tao rules,
Neither demons, spirits, nor sages
Can harm the people!

60.

Oatmeal Muffins To Go

Oatmeal or barley can be quickly baked into muffins, to be carried in one's backpack or satchel when riding trains or walking in the hills to visit Buddhist and Taoist monasteries. Food can be a problem when traveling on trains or in remote places. Monosodium glutamate and greasy foods are hard to avoid when the bus stops at a roadside stand for a quick lunch. A bag of raisin crackers or some oatmeal muffins provide a quick meal.

2 cups of flour
3/4 cup of rolled oats
1 tablespoon of baking powder
1 teaspoon of baking soda
1/2 teaspoon of salt, if desired
1/2 cup of vegetable oil or butter
1 cup of yogurt
1/2 cup of raisins, for flavor
2 tablespoons of water, if needed

Mix together all of the dry ingredients. Stir in the oil until the flour and oil are evenly mixed. Then add the yogurt and raisins, and stir until the batter is evenly mixed. The batter should be fairly stiff, but add a bit of water as necessary to achieve a good consistency (up to 2 tablespoons). Use a spoon to lay muffin-sized lumps of the batter on a sheet, and bake in the oven for about 20 to 25 minutes at 375°F, or until the top is brown. Allow to cool before packing them up for the road.

When traveling in China, one should always carry a 1-pint heat-resistant jar for making tea on a journey. Tea leaves are put in the jar, and hot water is added all day long, as a way of providing safe water for drinking. Although water safety is not a problem in the West, a thermos of hot water is a handy thing to carry. Have the muffins with green tea during your journey.

Lowest Is Best

The greatest country is the lowest,
Into which all things flow.
The feminine by nature stays calm,
And conquers the masculine.
Big or little, the lowermost wins.
Lowest is best.

Fried Rice

Since it is difficult to decide how much rice to make for a meal, especially when friends and other travelers tend to drop by to chat, the Taoist kitchen always has plenty of cooked rice ready for guests. Leftover rice can be fried in a tasty and healthy manner, an excellent dish to serve the late and hungry guest.

Fried rice is best made in a wok. To avoid having the grains become oil soaked, you should move the pan continuously in a circle, away from and then toward yourself while cooking, so that the ingredients are moved off the bottom of the pan before they burn while the oil remains hot in the center. This can be done quite well in a flat frying pan with a spatula, and, after a little practice, you will learn to move the frying pan in much the same to-and-fro circular manner.

3 tablespoons of vegetable oil
1/2 of an onion, finely chopped
2 garlic cloves, finely chopped
1 medium carrot, sliced into fine inch-long strips
1 cup of bean sprouts, if desired
1/2 small stalk of celery, finely chopped
4 cups of leftover cooked rice
1/2 teaspoon of salt,
or
1/4 teaspoon of finely chopped ginger

Heat the wok, and pour in about 2 tablespoons of cooking oil, the salt or ginger. When it is hot, first add the onions and garlic and stir-fry vigorously for about 1 minute. Then add all of the other vegetables, and stir again. Turn down the heat a bit, cover with a lid, and simmer. The liquid in the vegetables should provide sufficient moisture, but if not, add a little more oil. If more moisture is needed, add a tablespoon of water and cover again for 2 minutes. Finally, stir in the rice and continue stirring until the rice and vegetables are evenly mixed and the rice is not lumpy. Then, turn up the flames and stir vigorously for about 30 seconds. Remove the fried rice from the fire and serve hot.

The Best Gift

The Tao is hidden in small things.
When a king is crowned,
An official installed,
Jade and horses are given as gifts.
Best gift of all
Is closeness to Tao.

Tomato Sauce And Rice

Leftover rice can be prepared with tomato sauce and fresh tomatoes as an excellent dish for a truly meatless vegetarian meal. Canned tomato sauce from Xinjiang, made from tomatoes grown along the Silk Road in the Gobi and Taklimakan desert oases, is especially fragrant and makes a fine rice and tomato mixture. When it was prepared for a potluck dinner in Beijing, I found that it was the only dish that Uighur, Kazakh, and Hui guests would eat, fearing that the other Chinese dishes had been cooked in woks used for pork dishes. This rice goes well with any green vegetable recipes.

2 tablespoons of cooking oil
1 medium-sized onion, finely chopped
2 cloves of garlic, finely chopped
1/2 of a small can of tomato sauce (about 2 to 3 ounces)
1 cup of water
1 ripe tomato, chopped into 1/4-inch squares
4 cups of leftover white rice
1/4 teaspoon of salt (if desired)
1/4 teaspoon of cumin

Heat the wok and add the oil and salt. Stir-fry the onion and garlic until soft, covering the pot and letting them simmer for about 2 minutes. Mix about half of the tomato sauce with a cup of water and pour it into the wok, mixing well with the onions and garlic. Then add the fresh tomato and let this simmer until hot, for another 1 to 2 minutes.

Add the rice and stir until evenly mixed. Add the cumin, then let the rice and tomato sauce simmer together for about 10 minutes. Serve hot, with stir-fry vegetables, dried fruit, and nuts as complement.

Be Like Tao

Be like Tao,
(Wuwei, Transcendent Act)
Make little things important.
Make the few many,
Requite anger with goodness.
Tackle difficult things at once,
When they are easy.
Treat every job as difficult,
And all will be easy.

63.

Desert Fried Rice

Desert fried rice is served along the old Silk Road, from Lanzhou and Dunhuang in Gansu Province, Hami, Turfan, and Ürümqi in Xinjiang, to Tashkent and Samarkand. In its nonvegetarian form it is made with pieces of roast lamb fried together with the rice. The same ingredients, minus the roast lamb, make an excellent meal served by itself or with other condiments.

3 tablespoons of light cooking oil
1 medium-sized carrot, finely chopped
1 onion finely chopped
1 chopped long, thin green onion (jiu-cai), scallion, or some chives
2 cloves of garlic, chopped
1 tablespoon of sugar
1 tablespoon of tomato sauce or ketchup
4 cups of cooked rice
1/2 teaspoon of salt, if desired

Heat the wok and put in the oil and salt. Throw in the carrot, onion, garlic, and sugar, and stir vigorously for about 1 minute. Add the tomato sauce and let simmer for about 3 minutes at low or medium-low heat. Then add the rice and stir until the rice and flavored vegetables are evenly mixed. Turn up the heat, and continue to stir vigorously, making sure that the rice does not burn. Cook for another 2 to 3 minutes, until the rice is nicely heated.

A heaping plate of this fried rice, *juofan* in Mandarin, is served with nang bread and honey, brewed brick tea served in a rice bowl, and stir-fried vegetables. Uighurs and Kazakhs usually serve it with large chunks of roast or boiled lamb. A highly decorated dagger is used to carve the meat, and the rice and meat can be eaten with the fingers.

The hands are always carefully washed before and after eating. The washing of hands is an important ritual in the Xinjiang deserts. Not a drop of water is wasted. The guest is invited to wash his or her hands by the host, who pours the water from a silver pitcher. The guest receives the water in cupped hands and carefully rubs it over arms, face, and clothes, symbolizing purification before meals. When done, the hands are rubbed together until the water has evaporated. It is an insult to shake the water off the hands onto the ground.

Don't Scold

A huge tree began from a seed,
A tall building from a mound of dirt,
A long journey from my two feet.
Help each thing find its own way,
By not telling others what to do.

64.

Fancy Desert Rice

The Desert Fried Rice in recipe 63 can be prepared with a little fruit for variety. This manner of preparing rice can be found in southwest China as well as along the Silk Road.

3 tablespoons of cooking oil
1 medium-sized onion, finely chopped
1 chopped long, thin green onion (jiu-cai), *scallion, or some chives, for color*
2 cloves of garlic, chopped
1 medium-sized carrot, finely chopped
1 cup of long green beans (changdou), *thinly sliced*
1 cup of sweet fruit (apricot, peach, or pineapple), chopped
4 cups of cooked rice
1 tablespoon of ketchup

Heat the wok and add the oil. Stir-fry the onion and garlic for about 1 minute, then add the carrot and beans. Continue to stir-fry for about 2 minutes. Last, add the fruit, rice, and ketchup and stir until the ingredients are evenly mixed. Keep the mixture simmering for another 3 to 4 minutes. Stir occasionally so that the rice does not stick and the fruit does not burn. Serve hot, using fresh lettuce leaves as a colorful garnish. Sprinkle the chopped green onions over the top for color.

The Ancient Way

Of old, rulers who cherished the Tao
Taught the people simplicity,
Not how to be clever.
The erudite are hard to manage.
Forget cleverness, the country will be blessed.

65.

Mushroom Rice

Taoists believe that mushrooms are helpful for relieving high blood pressure and clearing harmful cholesterol from the blood. Only those who get migraine headaches are warned not to eat too many mushrooms. For most vegetarians they are an important part of the diet. Mushrooms bring a special flavor to rice when steamed together.

2 cups of washed uncooked white rice
5 dried mushrooms soaked for at least an hour in 2 cups of water
1 tablespoon of light cooking oil
2 cups of fresh mushrooms, chopped
2 tablespoons of light soy sauce
2 tablespoons of light sweet grape wine or cooking sherry

Wash the 2 cups of rice and let it soak in the cooking pot. Use the water used to soften the dried mushrooms for cooking the rice. Put the mushroom water into the electric cooker (or the pot for boiling rice). Chop the softened mushrooms into thin slices and add these to the rice pot. Cook the rice as directed in recipe 1. Add water so that it covers the rice to the height of the first joint of your index finger when the tip of your finger touches the top of the rice. Bring the water to a boil, cover the pot, reduce the heat to very low, and let it simmer for 20 to 25 minutes, until no more steam comes from under the lid.

When the rice is done, turn off the heat and let it sit for another 5 minutes. Heat the wok, and put in the oil. Add the fresh mushrooms and stir-fry for about 30 seconds. Then add the soy sauce and the wine. Simmer briefly, until the mushrooms are flavored but still fresh to the taste.

Put the mushroom rice on a plate and cover it with the cooked fresh mushrooms. Serve this dish with dofu and vegetables, and Cucumber and Tomato Salad (recipe 16).

The Great Ocean

Why is the ocean the greatest of all creatures?
Because it is the lowest.
Thus, all things flow into it.

66.

Eight-Jewel Fried Rice

The number eight is a symbol of blessing in the Taoist system. It stands for the eight trigrams of the *Yijing* (*I-ching*, Book of Changes), the orderly and timely changes in nature, and the Eight Immortals, Baxian (*Pa-hsien*), Taoist patron saints of medieval China. Vegetarian fried rice made of eight ingredients is therefore thought to be a propitious meal.

1/2 cup of diced carrot
1/2 cup of corn (canned corn is fine)
1/2 cup of sweet green peas
3 tablespoons of vegetable oil
1 pinch of ground black Chinese pepper, if desired
1/2 cup of finely chopped onion
1 long green onion or scallion, chopped into small pieces
2 cloves of garlic, chopped
1/2 teaspoon of sugar, if desired
1/2 cup of button mushrooms (enoki)
1/2 cup of straw mushrooms
1 tablespoon of light soy sauce
4 cups of cooked rice

First cook the carrots, corn, and peas in 2 cups of boiling water for about 2 minutes. Drain the water and put the parboiled vegetables into a bowl. Then heat the wok and add the oil. Put in the Chinese pepper (a bit of black pepper may be used instead). Add the onions, garlic, and sugar, and stir-fry for about 1 minute. Then add the peas, carrots, mushrooms, and corn. Reduce the heat and simmer for about 3 minutes. Stir in the soy sauce and the rice, mixing until the vegetables and rice are evenly distributed. Cover for another 2 minutes, and serve hot.

This dish makes a complete meal in itself. A fresh lettuce and tomato salad is a good complement.

Three Treasures

I have three precious things,
Kindness, thrift, and
Never preferring myself over others.
Heaven surrounds kindness,
Always coming to its aid.

67.

Sweet Eight-Jewel Rice

Sweet or glutinous rice is a popular dish in China, Japan, and Southeast Asia. It is much more nutritious than ordinary white rice, and much more filling. Sweet rice is served at most Chinese banquets as a kind of dessert, or for a change of flavor between main dishes. It can easily be found in Asian food supermarkets. Look for glutinous rice, or *mochi* rice, the Japanese term for the product. It must be soaked for at least an hour before using, and it requires a bit more time to cook.

There are three ways to use glutinous rice. It is cooked and served in place of white rice in southwest China, Thailand, and Laos. It is cooked with sweet red beans and pink food coloring in Japan (Jpn., *sekihan*). And it is steamed with eight kinds of dried fruit in China. This last dish is called *babao fan* in Mandarin, "Eight-Jewel Sweet Rice."

2 cups of glutinous rice
1/4 cup of mixed candied fruit (5 colors)
1/4 cup of chopped dates
1/4 cup of raisins
1/4 cup of cashew nuts, if desired
1/4 cup of finely sliced almonds

Wash the glutinous rice and soak it for an hour. Put it in the electric cooker or the pot used for steaming rice, and mix in the candied fruit, dates, raisins, and nuts. Be sure to wash any salt off the nuts before using them. Cover the rice with a little more water than used when cooking white rice. The water should be at least an inch over the surface. Bring the rice and fruit to a boil, then reduce the heat to the lowest possible flame and simmer for about 30 minutes, or until no more steam comes from the pot. If using an electric cooker, let it sit for 5 to 7 minutes after the cooking cycle has ended.

Put the cooked rice into 2 large rice bowls, filling each bowl to the top. Set aside until ready to use at the banquet. Before serving the rice bowl can be placed into boiling water and steamed until warm again. Turn the bowl of cooked rice and fruit out onto a plate, so that the top is rounded. The various fruits and nuts show through the glutinous rice, presenting a tasty and attractive dish.

No Contention

The best warrior doesn't fight,
A real winner has no enemies.
The best boss serves his workers.
Non-contention is a virtue,
One with the ancient Tao of heaven.

68.

Green Salad with Sesame Soybean Dressing

Some markets and mountainside gardens provide fresh lettuce for vegetarian meals. Eating uncooked vegetables can be dangerous throughout most of Asia, and lettuce that is to be eaten raw must be grown in a clean environment, where fertilizer, polluted water, and harmful bacteria do not contaminate it. If lettuce is to be used at a banquet, many Chinese prefer to cook it. Examine fresh lettuce carefully and wash it well in water with dish-washing detergent. Then rinse the leaves so no taste of detergent is left. In the West lettuce should be washed well to remove all dirt, but detergent is not necessary. Lettuce is used as a wrap for rice, dofu, and vegetables, and as a decoration for many vegetarian dishes. Dressing made from soybean paste, sesame seeds, sugar, and vinegar, completes an excellent dinner salad.

1 head of fresh, washed lettuce
1/4 cup of rice vinegar
1 tablespoon of sugar
1 tablespoon of sesame oil
2 tablespoons of brown soybean paste (miso)
2-3 tablespoons of water
1 tablespoon of roasted sesame seeds

Carefully clean, wash, and dry the lettuce. Put the vinegar, sugar, sesame oil and soybean paste into a bowl, and mix thoroughly. Add enough water to the mixture so that it can be poured over the lettuce. Heat a clean frying pan and roast the sesame seeds until they are brown and crisp, for about 2 minutes. Let them cool.

Arrange pieces of lettuce on each guest's plate, put a spoonful of the sauce over the lettuce, and sprinkle with the roasted sesame seeds. The sauce can be made milder or stronger by varying the amount of vinegar, water, and sugar.

Invisible Weapons

Better be a guest than a host,
Don't advance an inch and lose a foot.
Advance without moving,
Roll up sleeves without showing muscle,
Capture no enemy,
Hold invisible arms,
One who laments warfare wins.

69.

Silk Road Spaghetti

Many guests came to my kitchen in Beijing to sample, assist, and advise me in my study of Taoist cooking. The story of Marco Polo bringing spaghetti back to Italy from China prompted Uighur, Tibetan, Han Chinese, and Mongol friends to ask how the Italians ate noodles. We therefore created a spaghetti and tomato sauce dish consistent with the Taoist diet to offer as a surprise to guests who had never eaten foreign-style spaghetti. The following recipe is a variation of the tomato sauce made by relatives from the town of Trabia, near Palermo, Sicily. It does not use olive oil, and requires a little sugar to cut the acidity of strong tomato sauce. I had dried oregano leaves and found excellent Italian-style noodles in the markets of Beijing.

3 small cans of tomato sauce
2 large ripe tomatoes, cut into bite-sized pieces
2 cups of water
1 medium onion, finely chopped
5 garlic cloves, chopped
3 tablespoons of vegetable oil
1 laurel leaf
1 tablespoon of sugar
1 teaspoon of oregano
1 teaspoon of dried basil
1 teaspoon of salt
1 package of thin spaghetti noodles
Grated cheese, if desired

Put the tomato sauce, chopped tomatoes, water, and onion into a large pot and bring to a boil. Add about half the garlic, the oil, laurel leaf, and sugar, and let the mixture simmer over a low flame for about 45 minutes. Add the rest of the garlic, the oregano, and the basil, and simmer for another half-hour.

Meanwhile, put 2 quarts of water into a large pot, add a teaspoon of salt, and bring to a boil.

Put 1 package of thin spaghetti noodles into the boiling water and cook for about 12 minutes. One kind of white Chinese noodle cooks very quickly, in less than 3 minutes. Test the spaghetti regularly, to see when it is cooked al dente, that is, not too soft and not too hard.

If cheese is desired, a soft white cheese sold in many Beijing markets and stores throughout China, or Parmesan cheese, can be grated and sprinkled on top of each plate.

No Words

My words are easy to know, easy to do,
Because I have no words, no deeds.
Tao is ancestor of my words,
Lord of my deeds.
Thus I wear coarse clothes,
Hiding Tao deep inside.

70.

Uighur Pizza

The nang bread for sale in the Uighur restaurants and shops can be used to make an excellent pizza. Buy one or two of these round flat breads, freshly baked each evening, or use any bread that is available to you. Spread some of the tomato sauce from recipe 69 over a flat piece of bread. Add vegetables and mushrooms, some slices of the soft white Beijing cheese or mozzarella, and bake.

- 2 *round flat pieces of freshly baked nang bread (any bread will do)*
- 2 *cups of tomato sauce from recipe 69*
- 2 *cups of fresh chopped mushrooms*
- 1 *eggplant, sliced into small thin pieces*
- 1 *onion, sliced into thin strips*
- 2 *bell peppers, sliced into thin strips*
- 1 *package (8 ounces) of Beijing white cheese or mozzarella*

Cut the nang bread in half or into pieces that will fit into your oven. Cover the bread with tomato sauce. Then arrange the chopped mushrooms, eggplant, onion, and bell peppers on top of the bread. Sprinkle the chopped cheese on top for those who want it. Bake in the oven at 375°F for about 15 minutes or until the eggplant is softened. Serve hot.

Tao Is Not Known

Non-knowing is best.
Knowledge makes one ill.
I am sick of this illness called knowing.
The Taoist does not get sick,
Because he doesn't catch the "know all" sickness.

Fancy Vegetarian Cooking: Wheat Gluten

Many of the vegetarian recipes used in Taoist and Buddhist cooking are truly gourmet in quality. They require special ingredients and some experience to prepare. The following recipes were found at the Yuanxuan Xueyuan monastery in Kowloon. The ingredients can be purchased ready-made at Asian markets, but here is a simple way of making glutinous wheat cake, and other special Taoist dishes, for those who wish to try them. Most Chinese cooks know how to make these dishes and will probably be willing to serve them if they are asked for at a restaurant.

The first essential ingredient for fancy vegetarian cooking is wheat gluten, which takes the place of meat in many dishes. It is made as follows:

1 pound of flour
1 cup of water
1/4 teaspoon of salt, if desired

Pour a 1-pound package of flour into a pot with the salt and use enough of the 1 cup of water to make a firm, round ball of dough. Knead the dough until it does not come apart when handled.

Put the dough in the pot under a faucet with slowly running water and continue to knead the dough. Clouds of white starch will dissolve while you press and knead. When no more white starch comes from the ball of dough, wheat gluten remains.

Take this ball of wheat gluten dough and roll it into the shape of a sausage of a size that will fit into the pot. It can be put into a muslim cloth and tied at both ends, to keep it in the form of a sausage. Bring about a quart of water to a boil and cook the wheat gluten for about 20 minutes, or until it is firm and doesn't fall apart when pierced with a fork. Take the gluten out of the boiling water and let it cool.

The cooked wheat gluten can then be sliced into circular or semicircular pieces that resemble pieces of ham or chicken. Fry it in the wok with oil, garlic, and soy or teriyaki sauce, for "vegetarian ham" or "vegetarian chicken."

Value Self

When people don't fear you,
Your strength is greatest.
Don't meddle at home.
Don't be wearied of others,
And they won't weary of you.
Know your self, don't be self-conscious.
Love yourself, but don't be puffed up.

Fried Wheat Gluten Balls

Wheat gluten can also be made from dough mixed with yeast. Almost any bread recipe can be used; and the wheat starch is washed out after the dough rises a second time. I have not made the deep-fried wheat gluten balls myself because they are readily available in Beijing stores, and the strict Taoist diet avoids too much oil. I wrote down the following recipe while watching one of the cooks in the Yuanxuan Xueyuan kitchen. He began making the dough early in the morning, before breakfast, and it was used as a part of the vegetarian lunch.

1 teaspoon of salt
1 tablespoon (package) of dried yeast
2 cups of warm water
6 cups of flour
2 cups of vegetable oil for deep-frying

Mix the salt and yeast together with about 3 tablespoons of the warm water. Pour the flour into a large mixing bowl and blend in the warm yeast and salt. Knead for about 15 minutes, adding as much warm water as is necessary to make the flour hold together into a ball, then let the dough rise for about 3 hours. Punch the dough down and knead it into a large ball.

Kowloon is hot in summer, so the cook put the dough into the refrigerator for 2 hours. Removing the dough from the refrigerator, he put it into a pot under a tap of cold running water and kneaded it until no more starch came from the ball of dough.

He then took the ball and broke off small pieces, which he rolled into smaller balls about 3/4 inch in diameter. He heated 2 cups of oil in the wok until a drop of water sizzled on the surface and deep-fried the small balls of wheat gluten dough for about 5 minutes. They puffed up into 1 1/2-inch balls.

These balls were used as described in the following recipe (recipe 73).

Heaven's Net

The reckless cause slaughter,
The brave save lives.
Be like heaven's Tao,
Win without contention,
Answer needs without talking,
Come without being called,
Act without haste.
Vast and invisible is heaven's net.
Nothing gets by.

73·

Wheat Gluten Balls and Mushrooms

One of the most popular vegetarian dishes throughout China is made from wheat gluten balls fried with mushrooms, bamboo shoots, and carrots. The ingredients are similar to those used in preparing dofu and mushrooms, except that these ingredients are simmered for a few minutes in mushroom broth. This recipe comes from the kitchen of the Yuanxuan Xueyuan.

5 dried mushrooms soaked in 1 cup of warm water for 1 hour
1 medium-sized carrot, thinly sliced
1 cup of thinly sliced bamboo shoots
2 tablespoons of vegetable oil
1 teaspoon of sugar
1/4 teaspoon of finely chopped ginger root
20 deep-fried wheat gluten balls (recipe 72)
1 tablespoon of cornstarch to thicken the broth
3 tablespoons of mild soy sauce (to season)

Soak the mushrooms in a cup of warm water for an hour. Set aside the mushroom water and cut the mushrooms into bite-sized quarters. Cut the carrot into round or oval slices. The bamboo may be cut into thin triangles or inch-long julienne strips.

Heat the wok and put in the oil. When the oil is hot, add the carrot and bamboo shoots, stir-fry for about a minute, and then add 1/2 cup of mushroom water, the mushrooms, sugar, and ginger. Cover and let cook for one minute. Then add the wheat gluten balls and the rest of the mushroom water. Cover and let the mixture simmer for a good 5 minutes, until the carrot is soft.

Mix the cornstarch with 2 tablespoons of water and stir it into the mixture, cooking until it thickens. Serve this dish hot, over a bed of napa cabbage for decoration. A variation of this dish is made by using the white centers of napa cabbage instead of carrot. Use the green part of the leaves as a garnish.

Tao's Place

To try to take Tao's place,
Is like trying to cut wood
For a master carpenter.
Be careful, don't cut your hand.

74.

Baby Corn, Cauliflower, and Broccoli

Broccoli and cauliflower, when stir-fried with baby corn, make a fine-looking vegetarian dish on the Taoist menu. Canned baby corn is found in the Asian section of most supermarkets. The special sauce made for this recipe can be used on other vegetarian dishes.

8 pieces of broccoli broken from the stem
8 pieces of cauliflower broken from the stem
16 pieces of baby corn (from a can)
3 tablespoons of vegetable oil
1/4 teaspoon of ground Chinese pepper (huajiao)
1 teaspoon of chopped ginger root
2 garlic cloves finely chopped
1 tablespoon of chopped thin green onion or scallion
2 tablespoons of light white wine
1 teaspoon of cornstarch
1 tablespoon of soy sauce
1 teaspoon of sesame oil

Put the broccoli, cauliflower, and corn into a pot with boiling water and let them steam for about 1 minute. Save some of the water to make the cornstarch sauce later.

Heat the wok and add the 3 tablespoons of vegetable oil. First put in a pinch of the Chinese black pepper (or any mild black pepper), then add the chopped ginger, garlic, and onion, and stir-fry for about 30 seconds. Put in the cauliflower, broccoli, and baby corn, add the wine, reduce the flame, and simmer for about 4 to 5 minutes. Stir frequently so the vegetables do not burn.

Stir together the cornstarch, soy sauce, 2 tablespoons of the vegetable oil, and the sesame oil in a cup until perfectly smooth. Pour this into the wok and stir until the sauce thickens.

Remove the ingredients from the wok and arrange them on a plate, with the cauliflower in the center, representing Tao. Put the broccoli to the east, south, west, and north of the center, to represent the four seasons. Place the baby corn in rows between the broccoli. The corn pieces represent the four gateways of life, northeast (childhood), southeast (maturity), southwest (graceful aging), and northwest (the gateway to heaven). Pour the thickened gravy over the vegetables and serve while hot.

Taxes

Why do people starve?
Too many taxes.
Why do they break laws?
Politicans serve self-interest.
Provide plenty of good food to eat,
The people will value a peaceful life.

Eight-Jewel Vegetable Dish

Among the more elaborate dishes served at the Yuanxuan Xueyuan and other Buddhist and Taoist restaurants is a multivegetable dish that includes ginkgo nuts, water chestnuts, and *hoisin* sauce. Hoisin sauce (Mandarin: *haixian jiang*) is made of a sweet ground bean, sugar, and garlic. It is found in most supermarkets and can be added to any of the vegetable recipes as flavoring. The ginkgo tree is found throughout North America and the Asian continent. Its nutritious nut is found in the Asian section of many supermarkets. Substitute peanuts or cashew nuts if ginkgos cannot be found.

4 tablespoons of vegetable oil
1/2 pound package of dofu (7 to 8 ounces), cut into bite-sized squares
2 cloves of garlic, chopped
1 cup of green beans, destringed and halved
1 carrot, cut into round pieces
1/2 cup of straw mushrooms
1/2 cup of dried mushrooms soaked in at least 1 cup of water and chopped
1/2 cup of canned round button mushrooms
1/2 pound ginkgo nuts
8 pieces of baby corn
1/2 cup of canned water chestnuts
1 tablespoon of hoisin sauce
1 tablespoon of light white wine
1 tablespoon of cornstarch
1 teaspoon of light soy sauce
1 teaspoon of sesame oil

Put 3 tablespoons of the oil into a heated wok and brown the dofu on both sides. Set aside the browned dofu, and add the garlic, green beans, and carrot to the oil. Stir-fry, then simmer for about 3 minutes. Then add all of the mushrooms, the ginkgo nuts, baby corn, water chestnuts, hoisin sauce, and the wine. Simmer together for another 3 minutes.

Mix together a 1/2 cup of the mushroom-soaking water, cornstarch, soy sauce, and sesame oil. Pour this into the wok and let the mixture thicken, for about 30 seconds. Remove the wok from the fire, and arrange each ingredient on a plate. Pour the sauce over the top of the cooked vegetables.

Grass and Trees

Life is supple and yielding,
Death is hard and stiff.
Look upward, like living grass and trees,
Supple and tender.
Not downward, like dry stiff branches
Cut for kindling.

Lily Buds, Wheat Gluten, and Mushrooms

Lily buds are an important part of gourmet vegetarian diets. They are sold dried in most Asian markets. The same ingredients used in recipe 75 are used to prepare this health-giving dish.

2 tablespoons of light vegetable oil
1 clove of garlic, chopped
1 tablespoon of chopped ginger root
1 1/2 cups of both dried (soaked) and fresh mushrooms, as in recipe 75
10 deep-fried gluten balls
1 tablespoon of light white wine
1 tablespoon of hoisin sauce
1 cup of dried lily buds, soaked for an hour in water
1 cup of lily bud and mushroom-soaking water
1 tablespoon of cornstarch
1 tablespoon of light soy sauce
1 teaspoon of sugar
1 teaspoon of sesame oil

Heat the wok and put in 2 tablespoons of oil. Stir-fry the garlic, ginger, mushrooms, and deep-fried wheat gluten balls. Then add the wine, hoisin sauce, and 1/2 cup of the water used to soak the lily buds, the buds themselves, and mushrooms, and let this simmer together for about 3 minutes.

Mix the cornstarch, soy sauce, sugar, and sesame oil in the remaining 1/2 cup of lily bud water, and pour it into the wok. Stir for about 30 seconds, or until the sauce thickens. Serve this dish in a shallow plate, with freshly cooked rice.

Bend Like A Bow

Heaven's Tao is like a bow;
Pull the bowstring,
The top bends down,
The bottom bends up.
If the string's too loose, shorten it.
Too tight, loosen it.
Man's ways are different,
Taking from those who have little,
Giving to those who have plenty.
Be like the Tao,
Give of your plenty to all.

77·

Wines

The Western view of Taoism and some forms of Zen (*Ch'an*) Buddhism imagines a freedom-loving dissolute or "mad monk" who drinks to excess, is totally unrestrained, and follows whims with the changes of wind and weather. Nothing could be further from the truth. The Buddhist way of life is abstinent, and Taoists only serve wine or beer when guests come to eat and drink. Only the best wines should be served, in keeping with the Chinese custom of respecting and cherishing the visit of a friend.

One of the most popular and oldest forms of Chinese grape wine is the variety called China Red *Zhongguo Hong* (*Chung-kuo Hung*). This wine comes in a dark upright bottle with a red screw-on cap, red silk ribbon, and bright red-and-gold label. It is sweet to the taste, rather like a dessert wine or aperitif in the West, and can be served before or after meals to enhance a banquet, or warmed with orange peel and cinnamon as a remedy against the cold Siberian winds of winter. It can also be added to curry and vegetarian stews for flavoring.

Other excellent red and white grape wines are made in China that match the quality of French and Californian varietals. Some wines include a slightly sweet Beaujolais, a white wine called Great Wall, and a rosé wine from Xinjiang that can be bought at the Xinjiang Affairs Bureau.

When in China, always bring along a corkscrew if you bring wine to a party as a gift. Most Chinese wines have a metal screw top. The host may not have a corkscrew, and may use a chopstick to press the cork down into the bottle.

A Paradox

Nothing is softer or weaker than water,
Yet it overcomes the strongest and hardest....
The soft overcomes the hard,
The weak crushes the strong.
A paradox! Why not practice it?

78.

Beer and 100-Proof Alcohol

The drink of preference for the Taoist monk at a large banquet is beer, since the host and guest frequently compete with each other to see who can make the most toasts before experiencing a mild dizzy intoxication.

The *Daode Jing (Tao-te Ching)* warns the guest to know when to stop. The beers of Beijing, Nanjing, and Qingdao (Tsingtao) are truly world-class, brewed from the best yeast. Often each guest is given one or two quarts to consume during the banquet. Etiquette requires that beer be shared with the other guests at the table. Pour the beer generously into the glasses of those around you at the table, to maintain sobriety and good judgment.

Many of the preferred drinks at Chinese banquets are more than 100 proof, which is more than 50% alcohol. When liquor is poured into a guest's cup at a banquet, the guest is expected to drink the contents, even in small sips, unless he declares from the beginning of the banquet that religious (e.g., Buddhist practice) or health reasons forbid the taking of alcohol. If the guest accepts a first cup of strong spirits, everyone at the table will invite the unaware foreigner or scholar to down another cup.

In such cases it is possible to mix the strong white alcohol into a large glass of lemon-flavored soda or some other carbonated drink. Pour some of this soda back into the small cup each time it is emptied, to avoid incapacitation.

At other times one's cup will be refilled by the host or a nearby guest each time a toast occurs. When the toastmaster says "*ganbei*" (bottoms up), the simple reply, "*suiyi*" (just a sip, please), allows the guest to politely touch the liquor to his or her lips without drinking the whole cup.

No Favorites

The Tao of heaven plays no favorites.
It always stays with the good.
Goodness is a contract . . .
That puts no claims on others.
Tao and the Taoists have a contract,
Always to be one in goodness.

79.

Almond Pudding

Most Taoist households serve almond or apricot pit pudding, called *xingren dofu* (almond dofu). It is easy to make, and is served chilled after a fine meal.

1 package of clear, unflavored instant gelatin
1/2 teaspoon of almond extract
1 can of mixed fruit cocktail in light syrup or 2 cups of chopped fresh fruit (peaches, grapes, apricots, etc.)

Mix the package of instant gelatin and almond extract together with the required amount of water, as indicated on the gelatin package. Pour the mixture into two shallow (about 1/2 inch in depth), 6 x 8 inch pans, and put the pans into the refrigerator to chill.

Strain the juice from the can of mixed fruit cocktail. Pour the fruit (without its juice) into a large glass bowl, and put it to chill as well. After dinner, cut the gelatin into 1/4 inch cubes, and pour them into the bowl with the fruit. Mix gently so that the cubes don't come apart.

Tiny Kingdom

A Taoist's choice is a small country, . . .
Where the people don't travel too far,
Even though they have boats and carts.
No soldiers or weapons.
They eat and dress well,
Dwell peacefully in their homes,
Take joy in simple things.
The neighboring country is so close,
That they can hear dogs barking,
And cocks crowing. Yet,
All their lives,
They never go visiting.

80.

Candied Apples or Bananas

This dish, called *ba-si ping guo* (*ba-sz pingguo*, pull the thread apples) or *ba-si xiangjiao* (pull the thread bananas) is a favorite dish in north and northwest China. It requires about ten minutes to make and is a favorite dessert to serve after a vegetarian meal.

3 large or 4 medium-sized apples or 4 bananas
1 cup flour
2 cups of cooking oil, heated in a wok
2 cups of white, fine grain sugar
1/4 cup of roasted sesame seeds

Peel and cut up the fruit into bite-sized chunks, about 1/2 inch square. Put a cup of flour into a bowl and mix in water (about 3/4 cup to 1 cup) until it becomes a smooth light batter without lumps. The amount of water will depend on the humidity or dryness of the air.

Heat the oil in the wok until it just begins to smoke. Dip the apples into the batter, and use chopsticks to take them out and lay them in the oil. Deep fry the fruit until it turns an even light brown in color. Do not overcook the pieces—a crunchy warm consistency is preferable to a soft, gooey mess. When done, take the fried fruit out of the wok and lay it on paper or a wire wrack to drain off excess oil.

Pour the oil out of the wok and save it for later use. Then put the wok back on the fire and pour the 2 cups of sugar into the wok. Add about 2 tablespoons of water and let the sugar melt in the wok. When it begins to boil and light bubbles form on the surface, it is time to mix the melted sugar with the deep fried apples or bananas. Take a white serving plate, and pour a little cooking oil on the platter so that the melted sugar does not stick to the surface. Place the fruit in the center of the plate, pour the melted sugar on top, and sprinkle on the sesame seeds. Place a bowl of cold water on the table, into which guests should dip each morsel of fruit to cool it before eating. Threads of melted sugar will come up with the fruit as it is lifted off the plate—thus giving the dish its name of "pull thread apples." Crisp pears and even potatoes can be substituted for apples and bananas.

Giving Is Joy

Words in contracts are not beautiful,
Beautiful words are not found in covenants.
Good people don't dispute,
Disputes do not bring good.
Knowledge isn't always wise.
Wisdom isn't something learned.
The Taoist . . . finds joy in giving to others.
The more given, the more happiness.
Heaven's Tao gives,
Without harm or discord.

81.

Thank the Host and Go Home Early

Most families retire early after a banquet. Guests do not stay long after the last dish is served and the wife of the family has been helped to clean up and do the dishes.

In new China both men and women help with the cooking, and the men often do the dishes. The Taoist master joins the novices in the kitchen, helps make and serve the meals, and cleans the table after dinner.

Tea is always served after lunch and dinner. The guests are seen to the door or to the bus stop. A ride is provided home for those unfamiliar with the way. The Chinese sense of hospitality and welcome is reciprocated by the thoughtfulness and gratitude of the guest. Accepting an invitation to a dinner at home means the beginning of a lifetime friendship. Both the dinner and the friendship are to be cherished.

Index